face2face

Starter Student's Book

Chris Redston with Gillie Cunningham

Contents

Speaking	Listening and Video	Reading	Writing
Names Introducing people Phone numbers	Conversations at a party Phone numbers	Conversations at a party	
Names and countries What's his / her name? Where's he / she from?	**Help with Listening** Word stress Where are you from?		Sentences about people from different countries
First names and surnames Conversations in class	VIDEO ► Welcome to the class (1) and (2) VIDEO ► Classroom language	Conversations in class	
Talking about a photo What's in my bag?	What's in your bag?		
HELP WITH PRONUNCIATION /æ/ **and** /ə/ p13		**Reading and Writing Portfolio 1 Where are you from?** Workbook p52	
True or false?	Around the world	True and false sentences	True and false sentences
About your partner Tina's friends Six people	Photos of friends		yes / no questions
Good morning! Personal information	VIDEO ► The City Gym	Email addresses	Filling in a form
Questions with How old ... ? Guess the ages	**Help with Listening** Numbers with -teen and -ty Five conversations		
HELP WITH PRONUNCIATION /ɪ/ **and** /iː/ p21		**Reading and Writing Portfolio 2 Three people** Workbook p54	
Talking about two emails	**Help with Listening** Contractions	Two emails	
Your family	The Cooper family Our grandchildren	The Cooper family	Sentences about the Cooper family
Ordering food and drink in a café	VIDEO ► In a café	A price list in a café	
Food and drink	Fiona's family Food and drink I like	Food and drink I like	Sentences with love, like, eat, drink, a lot of
HELP WITH PRONUNCIATION /ɒ/ **and** /ʌ/ p29		**Reading and Writing Portfolio 3 See you soon!** Workbook p56	
True or false?	Life in Mexico Life in the USA	Life in Mexico Life in the USA	True and false sentences
Your free time Your partner's free time	An online interview **Help with Listening** Questions with do you	An online interview	Your free time yes / no questions
Buying things in a shop	VIDEO ► In a shop		A conversation in a shop
Film times	Days and times	Days and times	
HELP WITH PRONUNCIATION /θ/ **and** /ð/ p37		**Reading and Writing Portfolio 4 Internet profiles** Workbook p58	
Your daily routine Your partner's daily routine	Carol's routine Tom's routine	Carol's routine Tom's routine	
Nadine's routine Your best friend	Lunch on Monday **Help with Listening** Sentence stress (1)		Questions with does
Ordering food and drink in a restaurant	VIDEO ► In a restaurant	A restaurant menu	A conversation in a restaurant
Your Sunday routine	Our Sunday routines I love Sundays **Help with Listening** Sentence stress (2)	Our Sunday routines	True and false sentences
HELP WITH PRONUNCIATION /w/ **and** /v/ p45		**Reading and Writing Portfolio 5 My best friend** Workbook p60	

VIDEO ▶ See Teacher's DVD

Speaking	Listening and Video	Reading	Writing
A town or city you know	Susan's home town	Susan's home town	Sentences with *there is* / *there are*
Places near Susan's flat Places near your home	Welcome to my home **Help with Listening** Linking (1)		Questions with *Is there a … ?* and *Are there any … ?*
Asking for information at a tourist information centre	**VIDEO** ▶ At a tourist information centre	Two conversations	A conversation at a tourist information centre
Your clothes and colours Favourite things and people	My clothes	My favourite places	Questions with *your favourite*

HELP WITH PRONUNCIATION /tʃ/ and /dʒ/ p53   **Reading and Writing Portfolio 6** **A tourist in London** Workbook p62

Speaking	Listening and Video	Reading	Writing
Things you love, like, don't like and hate	We're very different	We're very different	Questions with *Does … like … ?* Questions with *Do you like … ?*
Things you and your family can and can't do	Help with the children **Help with Listening** *can* or *can't*		True or false sentences with *can* or *can't* Questions with *can*
Asking for and giving directions	**VIDEO** ▶ Directions	Conversations in the street	
Things you and your partner do online	An internet questionnaire	It's my internet!	

HELP WITH PRONUNCIATION /s/ and /ʃ/ p61   **Reading and Writing Portfolio 7** **The same or different?** Workbook p64

Speaking	Listening and Video	Reading	Writing
When I was ten	Three amazing days	Three amazing days	Sentences with *was* and *were*
When was she born? Your last wedding or party	An Indian wedding		
When's your birthday? Making suggestions	Dates **VIDEO** ▶ Happy birthday!		A conversation about next Saturday
Festivals in my town, city or country	Fantastic festivals Two festivals **Help with Listening** Linking (2)	Fantastic festivals	

HELP WITH PRONUNCIATION /ɔː/ and /ɜː/ p69   **Reading and Writing Portfolio 8** **Going out** Workbook p66

Speaking	Listening and Video	Reading	Writing
How you travel around The last time you visited a different town or city	**Help with Listening** Present Simple or Past Simple	Let's go by tuk-tuk! Around the world by bike	Sentences in the Past Simple
Things Heidi and Charlie did on holiday Your last holiday	Three holidays	Three holidays	Things you do on holiday Past Simple questions
Buying train tickets What you did last weekend	**VIDEO** ▶ At the station **VIDEO** ▶ Last weekend		Things you did last weekend
Questions about you and your partner	How many did I get right? **Help with Listening** Sentence stress (3)	A quiz	*Wh-* questions

HELP WITH PRONUNCIATION /l/ and /r/ p77   **Reading and Writing Portfolio 9** **On holiday** Workbook p68

Speaking	Listening and Video	Reading	Writing
Your future plans	Four students' plans	Four English students' plans	Sentences with *be going to*
Questions with *be going to* Students' future plans	Rosie's future plans		Questions with *be going to*
Saying goodbye and good luck	**VIDEO** ▶ See you soon!	See you soon! Two conversations	

HELP WITH PRONUNCIATION Vowel sounds: review p84   **Reading and Writing Portfolio 10** **Happy birthday!** Workbook p70

Phonemic Symbols p134   **Classroom Instructions p135**   **Self-study DVD-ROM Instructions p136**

1A ▷ What's your name?

Vocabulary numbers 0–12
Grammar *I, my, you, your*
Real World saying hello; introducing people;
phone numbers; saying goodbye

Hello!

1 a `CD1` 1 Look at the photo. Read and listen to conversation 1.

b `PRONUNCIATION` Listen again and practise.

c Practise conversation 1 with four students. Use your name.

d Tell the class your name.

> Hello, I'm Francesca.

> Hello, my name's Lee.

> Hi, I'm Youssef.

2 a `CD1` 2 Read and listen to conversation 2.

b `PRONUNCIATION` Listen again and practise.

c Practise conversation 2 with four students. Use your name.

HELP WITH GRAMMAR
I, my, you, your

3 a Fill in the gaps with *I* or *my*.

1 Hello, _I_ 'm Stefan.

2 _____ 'm fine, thanks.

3 _____ name's Emel.

b Fill in the gaps with *you* or *your*.

1 How are _you_ ?

2 Nice to meet _____ .

3 _____ too.

4 What's _____ name?

`GRAMMAR 1.1` ▷ p115

4 `CD1` 3 `PRONUNCIATION` Listen and practise the sentences in **3**.

5 a Fill in the gaps with *I*, *my*, *you* or *your*.

A

SUE Hello, _my_ name's Sue.
  What's _____ name?
MARIO Hello, _____ 'm Mario.
SUE Nice to meet _____ .
MARIO _____ too.

B

ADAM Hi, Meg.
MEG Hi, Adam. How are _____ ?
ADAM _____ 'm fine, thanks.
  And _____ ?
MEG _____ 'm OK, thanks.

b `CD1` 4 Listen and check.

c Work in pairs. Practise the conversations in **5a**.

Introducing people

6 a `CD1` 5 Read and listen to conversation 3.

b `PRONUNCIATION` Listen again and practise.

c Work in groups. Practise conversation 3. Use your names.

1
STEFAN Hello, I'm Stefan.
  What's your name?
EMEL Hello, my name's Emel.
STEFAN Nice to meet you.
EMEL You too.

2
TIM Hi, Anita.
ANITA Hi, Tim. How are you?
TIM I'm fine, thanks. And you?
ANITA I'm OK, thanks.

Numbers 0–12

7 **a** `CD1 6` `PRONUNCIATION` Listen and practise these numbers.

0 **zero**	7 **seven**
1 **one**	8 **eight**
2 **two**	9 **nine**
3 **three**	10 **ten**
4 **four**	11 **eleven**
5 **five**	12 **twelve**
6 **six**	

b Work in pairs. Say four numbers. Write your partner's numbers. Are they correct?

Phone numbers

8 **a** `CD1 7` `PRONUNCIATION` Read and listen to these questions and answers. Listen again and practise.

What's your mobile number?

It's 07954 544768.

What's your home number?

It's 020 7622 3479.

TIP • In phone numbers 0 = *oh* and 44 = *double four*.

b Work in pairs. Practise the questions and answers in **8a**.

9 **a** `CD1 8` Listen to three conversations. Write the phone numbers.

b Work in pairs. Compare answers.

3 NINA Polly, this is David.
POLLY Hello, David. Nice to meet you.
DAVID You too.

4 LUCY Goodbye, Miki.
MIKI Bye, Lucy. See you soon.
LUCY Yes, see you.

Get ready ... Get it right!

10 Work in pairs. Student A p86. Student B p91.

Goodbye!

11 **a** `CD1 9` Read and listen to conversation 4.

b `PRONUNCIATION` Listen again and practise.

c Say goodbye to other students.

1B **Where's she from?**

Vocabulary countries
Grammar *he, his, she, her*
Real World *Where are you from?*

QUICK REVIEW Phone numbers Write two phone numbers. Work in pairs. Say your phone numbers. Write your partner's numbers. Are they correct?

Countries

1 Look at the map. Match these countries to 1–12.

Italy [7]   Brazil [ ]   Russia [ ]   the USA [ ]
Germany [ ]   Egypt [ ]   Australia [ ]   Mexico [ ]
Turkey [ ]   the UK [ ]   China [ ]   Spain [ ]

⋮ HELP WITH LISTENING Word stress

2 CD1 ▶ 10 Listen and notice the word stress (•) in the countries in **1**.
Ítaly   Brazíl

3 CD1 ▶ 10 PRONUNCIATION Listen again and practise.

4 Work in pairs. Look again at the map. Say a number. Your partner says the country.

What's number 2?   Mexico.

Where are you from?

5 a CD1 ▶ 11 Look at the photo of Stefan and Emel. Listen to the conversation and fill in the gaps.

b CD1 ▶ 12 PRONUNCIATION Listen and practise.

c Where are you from? Tell the class.

I'm from Peru.   I'm from Libya.

I'm from Indonesia.   I'm from Prague.

d Work in groups. Ask other students where they are from.

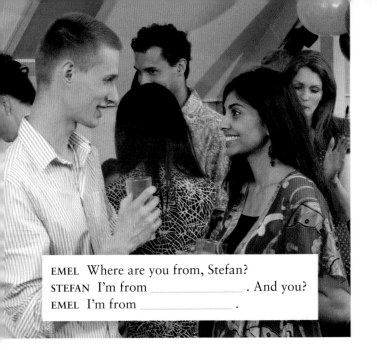

EMEL Where are you from, Stefan?
STEFAN I'm from _____ . And you?
EMEL I'm from _____ .

What's his name?

6 **a** Look again at the photo of Stefan and Emel.
Match questions 1–4 to answers a–d.

1 What's his name?   a He's from Russia.
2 Where's he from?   b His name's Stefan.
3 What's her name?   c She's from Turkey.
4 Where's she from?   d Her name's Emel.

b CD1 ▶13 **PRONUNCIATION** Listen and practise.

HELP WITH GRAMMAR *he, his, she, her*

7 **a** Fill in the gaps with *he* or *his*.

1 What's _his_ name?
2 _____ name's Stefan.
3 Where's _____ from?
4 _____'s from Russia.

b Fill in the gaps with *she* or *her*.

1 What's _her_ name?
2 _____ name's Emel.
3 Where's _____ from?
4 _____'s from Turkey.

GRAMMAR 1.2 ▶ p115

8 **a** Work in pairs. Look at A–F. Write sentences
about the people. Use these countries.

| ~~France~~ | Poland | Colombia |
| India | Thailand | Japan |

A His name's Marcel and he's from France.

b CD1 ▶14 Listen and check your answers.

Get ready … Get it right!

9 Work in pairs. Student A p87. Student B p92.

Paris

A

Ayumi

B

C

Warsaw

Tokyo

Leon

Marcel

Bangkok

D

E

F

Delhi

Bogotá

Gita

Mai

Ricardo

▶ REAL WORLD

1C

In class

Vocabulary the alphabet; things in your bag (1); *a* and *an*
Real World first names and surnames; classroom language

QUICK REVIEW What's his / her name? Work in pairs. Ask the names of students in your class:
A *What's his name?* **B** *His name's Marcus.*
A *What's her name?* **B** *Her name's Ana.*

The alphabet

1 CD1 15 **PRONUNCIATION** Listen and say the alphabet. Notice the **vowels** and the consonants.

Aa Bb Cc Dd Ee Ff Gg
Hh Ii Jj Kk Ll Mm Nn
Oo Pp Qq Rr Ss Tt Uu
Vv Ww Xx Yy Zz

2 CD1 16 Listen and write the letters.

What's your first name?

3 a Look at photo A. Then match the teacher's questions 1–3 to the student's answers a–c.

1 What's your first name, please?   a Ortega.
2 What's your surname?   b O–r–t–e–g–a.
3 How do you spell that?   c It's Pablo.

b VIDEO 1.1 CD1 17 Watch or listen. Check your answers.

Pablo   Sally

4 a VIDEO 1.2 CD1 18 Watch or listen to the teacher talk to two more students. Write their names.

1 D_____   K_____
2 _____   _____

b Work in pairs. Compare answers.

5 a CD1 19 **PRONUNCIATION** Listen and practise the questions in **3a**.

first name → *What's your first name, please?*

b Ask three students the questions in **3a**. Write their first names and surnames.

What's your first name?   It's Bianca.

Things in your bag (1)

6 a Work in pairs. Look at photo B. Match these words to things 1–9.

a **b**ag 1   a **d**ictionary ☐   an **a**pple ☐
a **p**en ☐   a **p**encil ☐   a **b**ook ☐
a **n**otebook ☐   an **u**mbrella ☐   a **m**obile ☐

b CD1 20 **PRONUNCIATION** Listen and practise.

7 Work in pairs. Look again at photo B. Say a number. Your partner says the thing.

> What's number 1?

> A bag.

HELP WITH VOCABULARY
a and *an*

8 Look at the words in **6a**. Then fill in the gaps in these rules with *a* or *an*.

- We use _____ with nouns that begin with a **consonant** sound.
- We use _____ with nouns that begin with a **vowel** sound.

VOCABULARY 1.5 ▶ p114

9 Fill in the gaps with *a* or *an*.

1 _a_ country
2 _____ number
3 _____ English dictionary
4 _____ student
5 _____ answer
6 _____ phone number
7 _____ Italian bag

Excuse me!

10 **VIDEO** ▶ 1.3 **CD1** ▶ 21 Look at photo C. Watch or listen to three conversations in class. Match students 1–3 to the words they ask about a–c.

1 Dorota   a Brazil
2 Pablo   b answer
3 Khalid   c pencil

REAL WORLD Classroom language

11 **VIDEO** ▶ 1.3 **CD1** ▶ 21 Watch or listen again. Tick (✓) these sentences when you hear them.

> Excuse me.
> What does answer mean?
> I'm sorry, I don't understand.
> What's this in English?
> Can you repeat that, please?
> I'm sorry, I don't know.
> How do you spell Brazil?

REAL WORLD 1.7 ▶ p115

12 **CD1** ▶ 22 **PRONUNCIATION** Listen and practise the sentences in **11**.

Dorota   Khalid   Sally   Pablo

C

13 **a** Fill in the gaps with these words.

> ~~Excuse~~   sorry   mean   spell   repeat
> What's   understand   know

A
PABLO ¹ _Excuse_ me. What does notebook ² _____ ?
SALLY Look. This is a notebook.

B
SALLY Do exercise 4 on page 10.
DOROTA I'm sorry, I don't ³ _____ . Can you ⁴ _____ that, please?
SALLY Do exercise 4 on page 10.

C
SALLY What's the answer to question 2?
KHALID I'm ⁵ _____ , I don't ⁶ _____ .

D
PABLO ⁷ _____ this in English?
SALLY It's an umbrella.
PABLO How do you ⁸ _____ that?
SALLY U–m–b–r–e–double l–a.

b Work in pairs. Practise the conversations. Take turns to be the teacher.

VOCABULARY
1D AND SKILLS ▶ People and things

Vocabulary people; things; plurals
Skills Listening: What's in your bag?

QUICK REVIEW **The alphabet** Write five English words. Work in pairs. Spell your words to your partner. Write your partner's words. Is your spelling correct?

1 **a** Look at the picture. Match these words to people a–e.

> a baby `a` a boy ☐ a girl ☐ a man ☐ a woman ☐

b **CD1 23** **PRONUNCIATION** Listen and practise.

2 **a** Look at the photo. Match these words to things 1–7.

> a diary `4` a chair ☐ a table ☐ a computer ☐
> a camera ☐ a watch ☐ a sandwich ☐

b **CD1 24** **PRONUNCIATION** Listen and practise.

c Work in pairs. What other things are in the photo?

3 **a** Look at the photo for one minute. Close your book. Write all the things in the photo you can remember.

b Work in pairs. Compare answers and check your partner's spelling. Who has more words?

HELP WITH VOCABULARY
Plurals

4 Look at these words. Write the missing letters.

SINGULAR	PLURAL
	+ -s
a chair	chair**s**
a table	table**s**
a thing	thing_
a boy	boy_
	+ -es
a wat**ch**	watch**es**
a sandwi**ch**	sandwich_ _
	y → -ies
a diar**y**	diar**ies**
a bab**y**	bab_ _ _
	irregular
a man	m**e**n
a woman	wom**e**n
a person	pe**ople**

VOCABULARY 1.8 ▶ p114

5 **CD1 25** **PRONUNCIATION** Listen and practise the plurals in 4.

6 Write the plurals.

1 a girl *girls*   6 a computer
2 a camera   7 a woman
3 a country   8 an apple
4 a watch   9 a dictionary
5 a man   10 a person

7 Work in pairs. Look at p96.

What's in your bag?

8 **a** `CD1` **26** Listen to three people in London. Tick (✓) the things in their bags.

A
books ✓
a dictionary
a computer
a notebook
pens
pencils
a mobile
a sandwich

Linda

B
a mobile
photos
a diary
a pen
books
an umbrella
an apple
sandwiches

Bill

C
a camera
a mobile
books
a watch
a notebook
pens
a pencil
an umbrella

Caroline

b Work in pairs. Compare answers.

c Listen again. Check your answers. Where are the people from?

9 Work in groups. Say what's in your bag. Ask your teacher for new vocabulary. Who has the same things?

HELP WITH PRONUNCIATION /æ/ and /ə/

1 `CD1` **27** Look at the pictures. Listen to the sounds and words. Listen again and practise.

/æ/
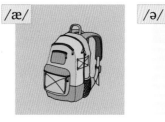
bag

/ə/

comput**e**r

2 `CD1` **28** Listen to these words. Notice how we say the **pink** and **blue** letters. Listen again and practise.

/æ/	/ə/
b**a**g m**a**n **a**pple	comput**e**r wom**a**n
pr**a**ctise voc**a**bulary	teach**e**r It**a**ly Chin**a**
th**a**t J**a**pan c**a**mera	Br**a**zil Jap**a**n c**a**mer**a**
underst**a**nd **a**lphabet	und**e**rst**a**nd **a**lph**a**bet

3 **a** `CD1` **29** Listen to these sentences. Listen again and practise.

1 Is your c**a**mer**a** from Chin**a**?
2 Your **a**pples are in my b**a**g.
3 Pr**a**ctise the **a**lph**a**bet.
4 My comput**e**r is from J**a**p**a**n.
5 Is he from It**a**ly or Br**a**zil?
6 Is your teach**e**r a m**a**n or a wom**a**n?

b Work in pairs. Practise the sentences.

continue2learn

▶ Vocabulary, Grammar and Real World
- **Extra Practice 1 and Progress Portfolio 1** p97
- **Language Summary 1** p114
- **1A–D** Workbook p3
- **Self-study DVD-ROM 1** with Review Video

▶ Reading and Writing
- **Portfolio 1** Where are you from? Workbook p52
  Reading four conversations
  Writing full stops (.) and question marks (?); capital letters (1); about you

Nationalities

1 **a** Write the missing vowels (*a, e, i, o, u*) in these countries.

1 *I t a l y*
2 B r _ z _ l
3 R _ s s _ _
4 the _ S _
5 G _ rm _ n y
6 _ g y p t
7 _ _ s t r _ l _ _
8 M _ x _ c _
9 T _ rk _ y
10 the _ K
11 S p _ _ n
12 C h _ n _

b Match these nationalities to the countries in **1a**.

a German *5*
b Mexican
c Italian
d Russian
e American
f Spanish
g Egyptian
h Brazilian
i British
j Turkish
k Chinese
l Australian

2 **a** CD1 30 PRONUNCIATION Listen and practise the countries and nationalities.

Italy, Italian

b Work in pairs. Say a country. Your partner says the nationality.

Turkey Turkish

c What's your nationality? Tell the class.

I'm Japanese. I'm French. I'm Colombian.

Around the world

3 **a** Work in pairs. Look at photos A–D. Fill in the gaps with a nationality from **1b**.

b CD1 31 Listen and check.

HELP WITH GRAMMAR *be* (singular): positive

4 Fill in the gaps with '*m*, '*re* or '*s*.

POSITIVE (+)

1 I____ British.   (= I am)
2 You____ a student.   (= you are)
3 He____ German.   (= he is)
4 She____ Brazilian.   (= she is)
5 It____ American.   (= it is)

GRAMMAR 2.1 ▶ p117

Hi, my name's Katy. I'm _____ .

His name's Dieter. He's _____ .

Her name's Luciana. She's _____ .

I'm Hector and this is my car. It's _____ .

5 [CD1▸32] [PRONUNCIATION] Listen and practise the sentences in **4**.

I'm → I'm British.

6 a Fill in the gaps with *'m* or *'s*.

1 She___ from São Paulo and she___ a student.
2 I___ from London and I___ a teacher.
3 It isn't a Mercedes. It___ a Chevrolet.
4 She isn't Australian. She___ from the UK.
5 He isn't from Berlin. He___ from Hamburg.
6 I'm not American. I___ from Havana, in Cuba.

b Work in pairs. Compare answers. Then match the sentences to photos A–D.

HELP WITH GRAMMAR *be (singular): negative*

7 Look again at **6a**. Then fill in the gaps in these sentences with *'m not*, *aren't* or *isn't*.

NEGATIVE (–)

1 I_____ American.   (= am not)
2 You _____ a teacher.   (= are not)
3 He _____ from Berlin.   (= is not)
4 She _____ Australian.
5 It _____ a Mercedes.

[GRAMMAR 2.2 ▸ p117]

8 [CD1▸33] [PRONUNCIATION] Listen and practise the sentences in **7**.

I'm not → I'm not American.

True or false?

9 a Check these words with your teacher.

the capital (city)   a singer   a company

b Work in pairs. Look at photos 1–10. Tick (✓) the true sentences. Make the other sentences negative. Write the correct sentences.

1 Madrid is the capital of Spain. ✓
2 Gisele Bündchen is German.
   Gisele Bündchen isn't German. She's Brazilian.
3 Leonardo DiCaprio is Italian.
4 Nissan is a Chinese company.
5 The Eiffel Tower is in Paris.
6 The White House is in New York.
7 Prince William is Russian.
8 Beyoncé is an American singer.
9 Fiat is a French company.
10 Beijing is the capital of China.

c Check on p134. Are your answers correct?

Get ready ... Get it right!

10 Work in new pairs. Write three true sentences and three false sentences.

Bill Gates is American.
BMW is a British company.

11 a Work in groups of four. Read your sentences to the other pair. Are the other pair's sentences true or false?

Bill Gates is American. | I think that's true / false.

Yes, you're right. / No, you're wrong.

b Tell the class two of your true sentences.

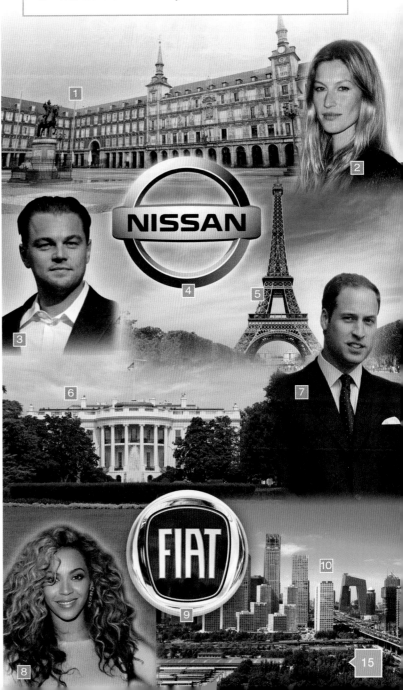

Jobs

1 **a** Work in pairs. Match these jobs to pictures a–i.

> a mánager **b**   a dóctor ☐   a téacher ☐
> a sáles assistant ☐   an áctor / an áctress ☐
> a wáiter / a wáitress ☐   a táxi driver ☐
> a músician ☐   a políce officer ☐

TIP • In these vocabulary boxes we only show the main stress (•) in words and phrases.

b **CD1 ▶ 34** **PRONUNCIATION** Listen and practise.

c Work in new pairs. Ask questions about the people in pictures a–i.

> What's his job?   He's a police officer.

> What's her job?   She's a doctor.

Photos of friends

2 **a** Check these words with your teacher.

> a friend   beáutiful   márried   síngle

b **CD1 ▶ 35** Look at the photo of Tina and Matt. Listen and match these names to photos 1–4 on Tina's computer.

> Sofia ☐   Marco ☐   Emma ☐   Gary ☐

c Listen again. Complete the table.

	Gary	Marco	Emma	Sofia
country	*Australia*			
job	*a doctor*			

HELP WITH GRAMMAR
be (singular): *Wh-* questions

3 Fill in the gaps with *am*, *are* or *'s*.

WH- QUESTIONS (?)

1 Where _____ I?
2 Where _____ you from?
3 Where_____ he / she / it from?
4 What_____ your name?
5 What_____ his / her name?
6 What_____ your job?
7 What_____ his / her job?

GRAMMAR 2.3 ▶ p117

4 **a** **CD1 ▶ 36** **PRONUNCIATION** Listen and practise the questions in **3**.

b Cover the table in **2c**. Work in pairs. Then take turns to ask and answer questions about the people in photos 1–4.

> What's his name?   Gary.

> Where's he from?   Australia.

> What's his job?   He's a doctor.

Tina　　　Matt

Is he a musician?

5 a Look again at the table in **2c**. Tick (✓) the correct answers.

1 Is Gary a musician?　　　**a** Yes, he is.　　**b** No, he isn't. ✓
2 Is Marco from Mexico?　　**a** Yes, he is.　　**b** No, he isn't.
3 Is Emma an actress?　　　**a** Yes, she is.　 **b** No, she isn't.
4 Is Sofia Italian?　　　　　**a** Yes, she is.　 **b** No, she isn't.
5 Are you from Russia?　　　**a** Yes, I am.　　**b** No, I'm not.
6 Is your watch Japanese?　**a** Yes, it is.　　**b** No, it isn't.

b Work in pairs. Compare answers.

HELP WITH GRAMMAR
be (singular): *yes / no* questions and short answers

6 Fill in the gaps with *am*, *are*, *aren't*, *is* or *isn't*.

YES / NO QUESTIONS (?)	SHORT ANSWERS
Am I in this class?	Yes, you are. / No, you _____ .
_____ you from Russia?	Yes, I _____ . / No, I'm not.
_____ he a doctor?	Yes, he is. / No, he _____ .
_____ she Italian?	Yes, she _____ . / No, she isn't.
_____ it Japanese?	Yes, it _____ . / No, it _____ .

GRAMMAR 2.4 ▶ p117

7 CD1 ▶37 **PRONUNCIATION** Listen and practise the questions and short answers in **6**.

8 a Fill in the gaps with *Is* or *Are*.

1　*Are*　you a student?
2　_____　your teacher from the UK?
3　_____　you Spanish?
4　_____　you married?
5　_____　your mobile in your bag?
6　_____　you a doctor?
7　_____　Beyoncé a singer?
8　_____　Leonardo DiCaprio a musician?

b Work in pairs. Ask and answer the questions. Use the correct short answers.

Are you a student?　　　Yes, I am.

Get ready ... Get it right!

9 Work in new pairs. Student A p87. Student B p92.

▶ REAL WORLD

2C

Personal information

Vocabulary titles; greetings
Real World email addresses;
personal information
questions

Good morning!

1 a Match 1–3 to a–c.

1	**Mr** (Brown)	a	a married woman
2	**Mrs** or **Ms** (King)	b	a single woman
3	**Ms** or **Miss** (Roberts)	c	a man (married or single)

b CD1 ▶38 **PRONUNCIATION** Listen and practise.

Mr → Mr Brown

2 a Look at pictures A–D. Complete the conversations with these phrases. Which three phrases mean *Hello*? Which phrase means *Goodbye*?

> Good morning   Good evening
> Good night   Good afternoon

b CD1 ▶39 **PRONUNCIATION** Listen and check. Listen again and practise.

c Work in pairs. Practise the conversations.

REAL WORLD Email addresses

3 Look at this email address. Notice how we say . and @.

eve.smith@webmail.com

> eve **dot** smith **at** webmail **dot** com

REAL WORLD 2.1 ▶ p117

The City Gym

Peter West
MANAGER
Tel: 0151 496 3211
1 email: peter.west@citygym.co.uk

The City Gym
12 Morton Street
Liverpool L8 3RF

email 12 of 26
2 frankrobson123@gmail.com
Subject: **Good morning!**

3 To: kimprice9@webmail.net
4 Cc: rebecca.taylor@email.org
Subject: meeting tomorrow

4 a Work in pairs. Say email addresses 1–4.

b CD1 ▶40 Listen and check.

5 a CD1 ▶41 **PRONUNCIATION** Listen and practise email addresses 1–4.

.co.uk → @citygym.co.uk → peter.west@citygym.co.uk

b Ask three students for their email addresses. Write the email addresses. Are they correct?

> What's your email address?   It's …

The City Gym

Karen

Peter

REAL WORLD
Personal information questions

6 Write the vowels (*a, e, i, o, u*) in these questions.

1 What's your f _i_ rst n _a_ m _e_ , please?
2 What's your s _ rn _ m _ ?
3 What's your n _ t _ _ n _l_ ty?
4 What's your _ ddr _ ss?
5 What's your m _ b _l_ _ n _ mb _ r?
6 What's your _ m _ _l_ _ddr _ ss?

REAL WORLD 2.2 ▶ p117

7 a **VIDEO ▶2** **CD1 ▶42** Look at the photo. Karen wants to join The City Gym. Watch or listen to her conversation with Peter. Tick (✓) the questions in **6** when you hear them.

b Watch or listen again. Complete form A.

A

The City Gym

New Member Form

first name   *Karen*

surname

nationality

address   *Road*

                    Liverpool

mobile number

email address

The City Gym, 12 Morton Street, Liverpool L8 3RF

c Work in pairs. Compare answers.

8 **CD1 ▶43** **PRONUNCIATION** Listen and practise the questions in **6**.

9 a Work in pairs. Interview your partner and fill in form B.

b Check your partner's form. Is it correct?

B

The City Gym

New Member Form

first name

surname

nationality

address

mobile number

email address

The City Gym, 12 Morton Street, Liverpool L8 3RF

QUICK REVIEW Numbers 0–12 Write the numbers 0–12 in words (*zero*, *one*, etc.). Work in pairs. Check your partner's spelling. Then say the numbers.

1 CD1 ▶44 PRONUNCIATION Listen and say these numbers.

13 thirteen	17 seventeen
14 fourteen	**18 eighteen**
15 fifteen	19 nineteen
16 sixteen	20 twenty

2 **a** Match these words to the numbers.

~~thirty~~   ninety   seventy   forty
eighty   fifty   a hundred   sixty

30 *thirty*	60 _____	90 _____
40 _____	70 _____	100 _____
50 _____	80 _____	

b CD1 ▶45 PRONUNCIATION Listen and practise.

HELP WITH LISTENING
Numbers with *-teen* and *-ty*

3 **a** CD1 ▶46 Listen to these numbers. Notice the stress.

fourteen   forty   sixteen   sixty   eighteen   eighty

b Where is the stress in these numbers?

seventeen   ninety   fifty   thirteen
thirty   nineteen   seventy   fifteen

c CD1 ▶47 Listen and check.

4 CD1 ▶46 CD1 ▶47 PRONUNCIATION Listen again and practise.

5 **a** Write the numbers.

21 *twenty-one*	24 _____	27 _____
22 _____	25 _____	28 _____
23 _____	26 _____	29 _____

b Work in pairs. Say these numbers.

27   35   49   52   68   73   86   94

6 **a** Write four numbers.

b Work in new pairs. Say your numbers. Write your partner's numbers. Are they correct?

7 **a** Look at the photo. Match these words to 1–5.

a girl ☐   a car ☐   a house ☐   a cat ☐   a dog ☐

b CD1 ▶48 Listen to five conversations. Fill in the gaps with the correct number.

a The cat is _____ .
b The house is _____ years old.
c The girl is _____ .
d The car is _____ years old.
e The dog is _____ .

8 **a** Fill in the gaps with these words.

~~How~~   is   are   I'm   old

¹*How* old ² _____ your house?   It's 100 years ³ _____ .

How old ⁴ _____ you?   ⁵ _____ thirty.

b CD1 ▶49 PRONUNCIATION Listen and check. Listen again and practise.

9 Work in pairs. Look again at photo A. Ask questions with *How old … ?*.

Amybeth   Richard   Lucinda

Adela   Dagmar

Joe   Alexander

Luke   Jessica   Maggie

Salvador   Alec   Belle

Jean   Don   Chris

10 **a** Work in new pairs. Look at the photos. Guess how old the people are. Use these ages.

| 2 | 3 | 5 | 13 | 16 | 22 | 24 | 35 |
| 41 | 47 | 51 | 58 | 71 | 76 | 80 | 87 |

I think Amybeth is 22.   I think she's 24.

b Check on p134. Are your answers correct?

HELP WITH PRONUNCIATION /ɪ/ and /iː/

1 **CD1 50** Look at the pictures. Listen to the sounds and words. Listen again and practise.

/ɪ/

/iː/

six   nineteen

2 **CD1 51** Listen to these words. Notice how we say the **pink** and **blue** vowels. Listen again and practise.

/ɪ/	/iː/
six thing his	nineteen he's she's
single Miss women	people please
British watches	Chinese police email
evening fifteen	evening fifteen

3 **a** Look at the vowels in **bold** in these words. Do we say /ɪ/ or /iː/?

it's /ɪ/   thr**ee** /iː/   sandw**i**ches   t**ea**cher
th**i**nk   marr**i**ed   **i**sn't   r**ea**d   mus**i**cian
ass**i**stant   m**e**   Span**i**sh   Japan**e**se   sixt**ee**n

b Work in pairs. Compare answers.

c **CD1 52** Listen and check. Listen again and practise.

---

continue2learn

▶ Vocabulary, Grammar and Real World

- Extra Practice 2 and Progress Portfolio 2 p98
- **Language Summary 2** p116
- **2A–D** Workbook p8
- **Self-study DVD-ROM 2** with Review Video

▶ Reading and Writing

- **Portfolio 2** Three people Workbook p54
  Reading business cards; addresses; forms
  Writing capital letters (2); filling in a form

QUICK REVIEW Numbers 1–100 Work in pairs. Count from 1 to 100 in threes: **A** *one* **B** *four* **A** *seven.* Then count from 1 to 100 in fours: **A** *one* **B** *five* **A** *nine.*

Adjectives (1)

1 a Match the adjectives to pictures a–h.

good | d | bad
hot | ☐ | cold
big | ☐ | small
new | ☐ | old
expensive | ☐ | cheap
beautiful | ☐ | ugly
friendly | ☐ | unfriendly
nice | ☐ |

b **CD1** ▶**53** **PRONUNCIATION** Listen and practise.

HELP WITH VOCABULARY
Word order with adjectives; *very*

2 a Read these rules about adjectives.

- **Adjectives** go after **be**: *Your watch is nice.*
- **Adjectives** go before **nouns**: *It's a new car.*
- **Adjectives** are <u>not</u> plural with **plural nouns**: *They're good friends.*

b Look at the pictures and read the sentences. Then read the rule.

It's hot.   It's very hot.

- We put **very** before **adjectives**: *It's very hot.*

VOCABULARY 3.2 ▶ **p118**

3 Make sentences with these words.

1 a / It's / computer / old / very .
It's a very old computer.
2 a / He's / good / very / actor .
3 an / camera / It's / expensive .
4 very / nice / friends / are / His .
5 good / musician / a / She's .
6 is / very / house / beautiful / Her .
7 a / It's / night / cold / very .
8 friendly / children / Your / very / are .

An email to friends

4 a Work in pairs. Do you know these words?

a hotel	a room	a restaurant
a café	a mosque	a museum

b Check new words in **4a** with your teacher.

c Read email A. Where are Alice and Mike?

A

Hi Liz and Steve

How are you? We're in Istanbul and it's very hot here! Istanbul is a beautiful city and the people are very friendly. The restaurants are good and they aren't very expensive. We're in a small hotel near the Blue Mosque. The rooms are nice and they're very big. We aren't in the hotel now, we're in a café. Where are you? Are you in London?

Love Alice and Mike

5 Read email A again. Tick (✓) the true sentences. Change the adjectives in the false sentences.

      hot
1 It's very ~~cold~~ in Istanbul.
2 Istanbul is a beautiful city. ✓
3 The people are unfriendly.
4 The restaurants are good.
5 Alice and Mike are in a big hotel.
6 The hotel rooms are nice.
7 The rooms are very small.

HELP WITH GRAMMAR
be (plural): positive and negative

6 Fill in the gaps with *'re* or *aren't*.

POSITIVE (+)

We _____ in a small hotel. (= we are)
You *'re* from the UK. (= you are)
They _____ very big. (= they are)

NEGATIVE (−)

We _____ in the hotel now. (= are not)
You *aren't* from Turkey.
They _____ very expensive.

TIPS • With plural nouns we write *people are* not ~~*people're*~~, *rooms are* not ~~*rooms're*~~, etc.
• *You* is singular and plural: *You're* **a** *student. You're students*.

`GRAMMAR 3.1` ▸ p119

7 `CD1` ▸ 54 `PRONUNCIATION` Listen and practise the sentences in **6**.

HELP WITH LISTENING Contractions

8 a `CD1` ▸ 55 Listen and write the contractions (*I'm, we're, aren't*, etc.).

1 We *aren't* from Italy, _____ from Spain.
2 _____ a new hotel, but it _____ very nice.
3 _____ a doctor and he _____ married.
4 You _____ Australian, _____ American.
5 _____ a manager and _____ a musician.
6 _____ actors, but they _____ very good.

b Work in pairs. Compare answers.

9 `CD1` ▸ 55 `PRONUNCIATION` Listen again and practise the sentences in **8a**.

Where are they?

10 Read email B. Where are Liz and Steve? Then choose the correct words.

Hi Alice and Mike

Thanks for your email. Steve and I ¹*isn't* / *aren't* in London now, we ²*'s* / *'re* in Cairo! It ³*'s* / *'re* a very beautiful city. The people ⁴*is* / *are* very friendly and the restaurants ⁵*isn't* / *aren't* very expensive. We ⁶*'re* / *'s* in a big hotel near the Egyptian Museum. The rooms ⁷*is* / *are* very nice, but the hotel ⁸*isn't* / *aren't* cheap. It ⁹*'s* / *'re* very hot here too!

Love Liz and Steve

HELP WITH GRAMMAR
be (plural): questions and short answers

11 Fill in the gaps with *are* or *aren't*.

QUESTIONS (?)	SHORT ANSWERS
Are we in room 216?	Yes, you are. No, you _____ .
_____ you in London?	Yes, we _____ . No, we aren't.
_____ they in a big hotel?	Yes, they are. No, they _____ .
Where _____ we / you / they? Where _____ Liz and Steve?	

`GRAMMAR 3.2` ▸ p119

12 `CD1` ▸ 56 `PRONUNCIATION` Listen and practise the questions and short answers in **11**.

> ## Get ready ... Get it right!
> **13** Work in pairs. Student A p88. Student B p93.

3B ► **Brothers and sisters**

Vocabulary family
Grammar possessive 's; subject pronouns
(*I, you*, etc.) and possessive adjectives
(*my, your*, etc.)

QUICK REVIEW Adjectives Write four adjectives. Work in pairs. Take turns to say an adjective from your list. Your partner says the opposite adjective: **A** *new* **B** *old*. Then say one thing for each adjective: **A** *a new car* **B** *an old computer*.

1 My name's Nick. Fiona's my **wife**. Kevin's our **son** and Anne's our **daughter**.

2 My name's Fiona. Nick's my **husband**. Anne and Kevin are our **children**.

3 My name's Kevin. Nick's my **father** and Fiona's my **mother**. Anne's my **sister**.

4 My name's Anne. Kevin's my **brother**. Fiona and Nick are my **parents**. I call them **mum** and **dad**.

Our family

1 CD1 ► 57 Look at the photo. Read and listen to the Cooper family.

2 **a** Work in pairs. Look again at the photo. Then complete the table with words in bold in 1–4.

🧍 men / boys	🧍 women / girls	🧍🧍 both
father (_____)	(mum)	_____
_____	daughter	(singular: **child**)
husband	_____	
_____	sister	

b CD1 ► 58 **PRONUNCIATION** Listen and practise.

3 Choose the correct words.

1 Nick is Fiona's *son* / *husband*.
2 Kevin is Nick's *brother* / *son*.
3 Fiona is Kevin's *mother* / *daughter*.
4 Anne is Fiona's *sister* / *daughter*.
5 Nick is Anne's *brother* / *father*.
6 Anne is Kevin's *mother* / *sister*.
7 Nick and Fiona are Kevin and Anne's *children* / *parents*.

HELP WITH GRAMMAR Possessive *'s*

4 Read the rule.

● We use a name (*Nick*, etc.) or a noun for a person (*sister*, etc.) + **'s** for the possessive.
Fiona is Nick's wife. It's my sister's car.

TIP • **'s** can mean *is* or **the possessive**: *Anne's my sister.* (*'s* = is); *Kevin is Nick's son.* (*'s* = possessive).

GRAMMAR 3.3 ► p119

5 CD1 ► 59 **PRONUNCIATION** Listen and practise the sentences in **3**.

6 Make sentences about these people.

1 Nick → Kevin   *Nick is Kevin's father.*
2 Fiona → Nick
3 Kevin → Fiona
4 Anne → Nick
5 Kevin → Anne
6 Anne and Kevin → Nick and Fiona

Our grandchildren

Sid

Mary

7 **a** Look at the photo. Sid and Mary are Kevin and Anne's grandparents. Then write these words in the table.

| grandparents | grandson | grandmother |

	grandfather	
		granddaughter
		grandchildren

b CD1▸60 **PRONUNCIATION** Listen and practise.

8 **a** CD1▸61 Listen to Mary talk about her family. Put these people in the order she talks about them (1–5).

| Sid *1* | Anne ☐ | Fiona ☐ | Kevin ☐ | Nick ☐ |

b Listen again. Answer these questions.

1 How old is Sid?   *He's 64.*
2 What is Fiona's job?
3 How old is Fiona?
4 What is Nick's job?
5 Is Anne a good musician?
6 How old is Kevin?

HELP WITH GRAMMAR Subject pronouns (*I*, *you*, etc.) and possessive adjectives (*my*, *your*, etc.)

9 **a** Look at these sentences. Then complete the table with the words in blue and pink.

I'm Mary and this is Sid, **my** husband.
Her husband's name is Nick and **he**'s a doctor.
These are **their** two children – **our** grandchildren.
It's a very nice photo, I think.

subject pronouns		you		she		we	they
possessive adjectives		**your**	his		its		

b Are these words verbs (V) or nouns (N)?

| be *V*   sister *N*   family ☐ |
| listen ☐   read ☐   cat ☐ |

c Read these rules.

● We use **subject pronouns** with verbs (*I'm*, *you listen*, *they read*, etc.).
● We use **possessive adjectives** with nouns (*my sister*, *your family*, *their cat*, etc.).

GRAMMAR 3.4 ▸ p119

10 Choose the correct words.

1 Excuse me. Is this *you / your* dictionary?
2 *They / Their* aren't with *they / their* parents.
3 This is *we / our* cat. *He / His* name's Prince.
4 *I / My* friend Charlotte is from *you / your* city.
5 Are *you / your* at *he / his* house now?
6 *She / Her* brother's a teacher, but *she / her* isn't.

Get ready ... Get it right!

11 Write the names of people in your family.

12 **a** Work in pairs. Tell your partner about the people in your family. Ask questions about the people in your partner's family.

Pedro is my brother.   How old is he?

He's 29.   What's his job?

He's a waiter.   Is he married?

b Tell the class about one person in your partner's family.

Pedro is Carola's brother. He's 29 and he's a waiter. He's ...

3C ▶ REAL WORLD Eat in or take away?

Vocabulary food and drink (1)
Real World money and prices;
How much … ?; in a café

Money and prices

1 a Match prices 1–6 to a–f.

1	£10	a	ten dollars
2	10p	b	ten p (= pence)
3	£10.50	c	ten euros
4	€10	d	ten cents
5	$10	e	ten (pounds) fifty
6	10c	f	ten pounds

b CD1 62 PRONUNCIATION Listen and practise.

2 a Work in pairs. Say these prices.

£17 · 70p · $100 · €21 · $21.50 · 35c · €3.75 · £7.60

b CD1 63 PRONUNCIATION Listen and check. Listen again and practise.

3 a CD1 64 Listen to five conversations. Write the prices.

b Work in pairs. Compare answers.

REAL WORLD *How much … ?*

4 Fill in the gaps with *is* or *are*.

SINGULAR
1 How much _____ this watch?
2 How much _____ it?

PLURAL
3 How much _____ the pens?
4 How much _____ they?

REAL WORLD 3.2 ▶ p119

5 CD1 65 PRONUNCIATION Listen and practise the questions in **4**.

★ Café Pronto ★
PRICE LIST

★ Drinks ★
coffee £1.95
cappuccino £2.30
espresso £1.75
tea £1.60
mineral water £1.55
orange juice £1.90

★ Food ★
croissant £1.55
egg sandwich £2.45
cheese and tomato sandwich £2.65
tuna salad £3.50

Can I help you?

6 a Look at the price list. Match the food and drink to photos 1–10.

b CD1 66 PRONUNCIATION Listen and practise the food and drink on the price list.

c Work in pairs. Look again at photos 1–10. Test your partner.

What's number 1?   A cheese and tomato sandwich.

7 Look again at the price list. Work in new pairs. Choose food and drink. Ask your partner the price.

How much is an espresso and a croissant?   Three pounds thirty.

8 a VIDEO 3 CD1 67 Look at the photo of Café Pronto. Then watch or listen to two customers. Tick (✓) what they order on the price list.

b Watch or listen again. How much does each customer spend?

REAL WORLD *In a café*

9 Read the conversation. Fill in the gaps with these words.

~~help~~   very   away   please   thanks   in

ASSISTANT

Can I ¹*help* you?

Sure. Anything else?

Eat in or take ⁴_____?

OK, that's (£8.60), please.

You're welcome.

CUSTOMER

Yes, (two cappuccinos), ²_____.

Yes, (a croissant and an egg sandwich), please.

No, that's all, ³_____.

Eat ⁵_____, please.

Take away, please.

Thank you ⁶_____ much.

Thanks a lot.

REAL WORLD 3.3 ▶ **p119**

10 a **CD1** ▶ **68** **PRONUNCIATION** Listen and practise the sentences in **9**.

b Work in pairs. Practise the conversation in **9**. Take turns to be the customer.

11 a Work in new pairs. Look again at the price list. Take turns to order food and drink.

b Role-play a conversation for the class.

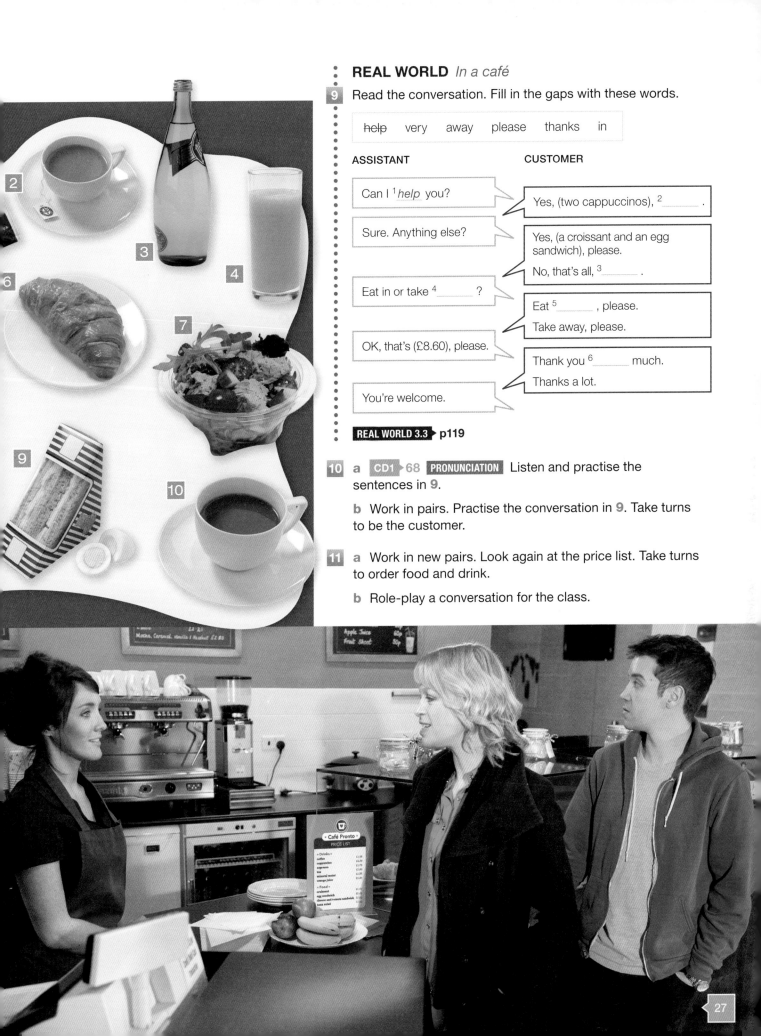

Vocabulary food and drink (2); *love, like, eat, drink, a lot of*
Skills Listening: Fiona's family; Reading and Listening: food and drink I like

QUICK REVIEW Money and prices Write four prices ($55, £10.50, etc.). Work in pairs. Say your prices. Write your partner's prices. Are they correct?

1 a Work in pairs. Look at the photo. Match these words to 1–16.

coffee 3	milk	tea	sugar	meat	fish
orange juice	eggs	cheese	bread	pasta	
rice	vegetables	fruit	chocolate	water	

b **CD1** 69 **PRONUNCIATION** Listen and practise.

2 a Look at the photo for one minute. Remember the food and drink.

b Close your books. Work in pairs. Say all the food and drink in the photo.

3 Match sentences 1–4 to pictures A–D.

1 I **like** fish. *B*
2 I **love** chocolate.
3 I **drink a lot of** coffee.
4 I **eat a lot of** rice.

4 **CD1** 70 **PRONUNCIATION** Listen and practise the sentences in **3**.

5 a **CD1** 71 Listen to Fiona. Tick (✓) the food and drink in **1a** she talks about.

b Listen again. Choose the correct words.

1 Nick is Fiona's (husband) / son.
2 Fiona and Nick love *coffee / milk*.
3 They drink a lot of *water / tea*.
4 They eat a lot of *meat / fish*.
5 Anne and Kevin like *eggs / cheese*.
6 They also eat a lot of *vegetables / pasta*.
7 They love *fruit / chocolate*.

c Work in pairs. Compare answers.

6 a Check these words with your teacher.

> a cup (of coffee)   a litre   ice cream
> biscuits   a vegetarian

b Read about Zoe, Ed, Mei and Ben. Fill in the gaps with their names.

1 _Zoe_ and _Ben_ like rice and pasta.
2 _____ and _____ eat a lot of sandwiches.
3 _____ and _____ drink a lot of coffee.
4 _____ and _____ love salads.
5 _____ and _____ eat a lot of fruit.
6 _____ and _____ like chocolate biscuits.
7 _____ and _____ love ice cream.

ZOE I love coffee and I drink four or five cups a day. I also drink a lot of water, about two litres a day. I like rice and pasta, and I eat a lot of salads and vegetables. I also like French cheese, and I love Italian ice cream!

ED I drink a lot of coffee, but I like it black, not with milk. I also like chocolate biscuits with my coffee. I eat a lot of meat and fish, but not fruit or vegetables. And I eat a lot of bread – I love egg sandwiches.

MEI In the morning I drink tea, not coffee. I eat a lot of rice, fish and vegetables, of course. I love apples and oranges, and I eat a lot of cheese sandwiches. But I also eat a lot of chocolate biscuits in the evening!

BEN I'm a vegetarian, so I eat a lot of fruit and vegetables, but not meat or fish. I also like rice and pasta, and I love salads. I drink a lot of fruit juice – people say it's very good for you. And I love chocolate ice cream!

7 a **CD1 ▶72** Listen to Zoe, Ed, Mei and Ben. Underline all the food words.

b Work in pairs. Compare answers.

8 a Write six sentences about you. Use *love, like, eat, drink, a lot of* and words from **1a**.

I eat a lot of pasta.

b Work in groups. Say your sentences. Do you like the same things?

HELP WITH PRONUNCIATION /ɒ/ and /ʌ/

1 **CD1 ▶73** Look at the pictures. Listen to the sounds and words. Listen again and practise.

/ɒ/	/ʌ/

c**o**ffee	**u**mbrella

2 **CD1 ▶74** Listen to these words. Notice how we say the **pink** and **blue** vowels. Listen again and practise.

/ɒ/	/ʌ/
c**o**ffee d**o**g d**o**ctor	**u**mbrella m**u**ch
h**o**t w**a**tch ch**o**colate	n**u**mber c**ou**ntry
orange wr**o**ng	m**o**ther s**o**n br**o**ther
d**o**llar sh**o**p	h**u**sband l**o**ve m**o**ney

3 a Work in pairs. Cover **2**. Then look at the vowels in bold. Which vowel sound is different?

1 h**o**t   **o**range   (m**u**ch)
2 m**o**ther   d**o**ctor   s**o**n
3 d**o**llar   c**ou**ntry   m**o**ney
4 d**o**g   ch**o**colate   l**o**ve
5 sh**o**p   n**u**mber   br**o**ther
6 w**a**tch   h**u**sband   wr**o**ng

b **CD1 ▶75** Listen and check. Listen again and practise.

---

continue2learn

▶ Vocabulary, Grammar and Real World

- **Extra Practice 3 and Progress Portfolio 3** p99
- **Language Summary 3** p118
- **3A–D** Workbook p13
- **Self-study DVD-ROM 3** with Review Video

▶ Reading and Writing

- **Portfolio 3** See you soon! Workbook p56
  Reading holiday emails
  Writing apostrophes; *and* and *but*; a holiday email

Vocabulary phrases with *like, have, live, work, study*
Grammar Present Simple (*I, you, we, they*): positive and negative

Phrases with *like, have, live, work, study*

1 **a** Match these words or phrases to the verbs.

~~football~~	two children	English	in a flat
for a Spanish company	rock music	languages	
in the centre of the city	a car	in an office	

TIP • a flat (UK) = an apartment (US)

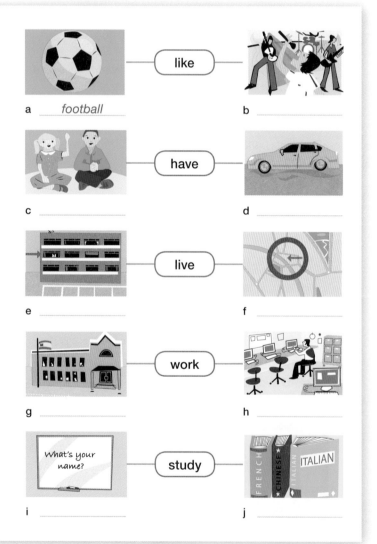

a   *football*

b   _____

like

c   _____

d   _____

have

e   _____

f   _____

live

g   _____

h   _____

work

i   _____

j   _____

study

b CD2 ▶1 **PRONUNCIATION** Listen and practise.

c Work in pairs. Test your partner on the phrases in **1a**.

languages   study languages

Life in Mexico

2 **a** CD2 ▶2 Read and listen to Carmen. Who are Cesar, Marissa and Teresa?

b Read about Carmen again. Choose the correct words.

1 Carmen is *single* / (*married*) .
2 She's *Mexican* / *Colombian*.
3 Carmen and Cesar live in *Mexico City* / *Mérida*.
4 Carmen's phone is *two* / *three* years old.
5 Their flat *is* / *isn't* in the centre of the city.
6 Their daughters *are* / *aren't* very good at English.
7 They like *Italian* / *Chinese* food.

c Work in pairs. Compare answers.

Hello, my name's Carmen. I'm married and my husband's name is Cesar. We're from Mexico, but we don't live in Mexico City. We live in a city called Mérida. I work for a mobile phone company, but I don't have a new phone. My phone is three years old! We live in a very nice flat in the centre of the city and we have two daughters, Marissa and Teresa. Marissa's nine and Teresa's twelve. They both study English at school – they're very good. They like rock music, football and Italian food, but they don't like Chinese food – or homework!

Carmen

Present Simple (*I, you, we, they*): positive and negative

3 **a** <u>Underline</u> the verbs in these sentences. They are in the Present Simple.

POSITIVE (+)

I <u>work</u> for a mobile phone company.
You study English.
We live in a very nice flat.
They like rock music.

b Look at these sentences. Notice the word order.

NEGATIVE (−)

I	don't	have	a new phone.	(**don't** = do not)
You	don't	study	Russian.	

c Write these sentences in the table.

1 We **don't live** in Mexico City.
2 They **don't like** Chinese food.

TIP • The Present Simple positive and negative are the same for *I, you, we* and *they*.

GRAMMAR 4.1 ▶ p121

4 CD2 ▶ 3 PRONUNCIATION Listen and practise the sentences in **3**.

Life in the USA

5 **a** Read about Richard. Fill in the gaps with the positive (+) or negative (−) form of *like, have, live, work* or *study*.

b CD2 ▶ 4 Listen and check your answers.

6 **a** Tick (✓) the sentences that are true for you. Make the other sentences negative.

1 I live in the centre of the city.
   I don't live in the centre of the city.
2 I work in an office.
3 I like Italian food.
4 I like rock music.
5 I have a new computer.
6 I have a sister.
7 I study English.
8 I live in a small house.
9 I work for an American company.

b Work in pairs. Compare sentences. How many are the same?

Get ready … Get it right!

7 Write three true sentences and three false sentences about you. Use phrases from **1a** or your own ideas.

I don't like rock music.
I live in a very small flat.
I work in a restaurant.

8 Work in new pairs. Say your sentences. Are your partner's sentences true or false?

I don't like rock music.

I think that's true / false.

Yes, you're right. / No, you're wrong.

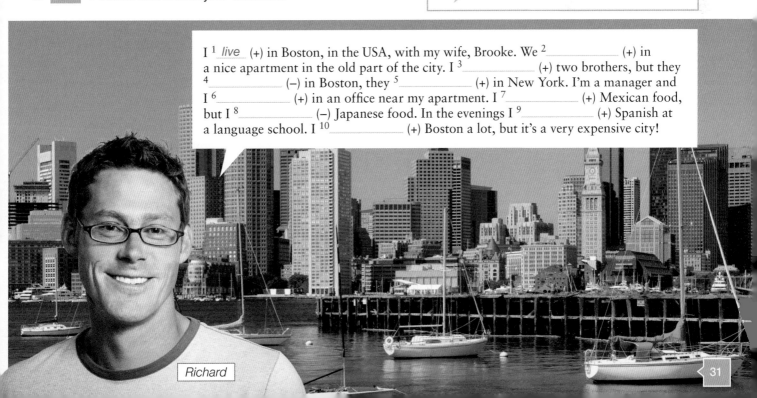

I ¹ *live* (+) in Boston, in the USA, with my wife, Brooke. We ² _____ (+) in a nice apartment in the old part of the city. I ³ _____ (+) two brothers, but they ⁴ _____ (−) in Boston, they ⁵ _____ (+) in New York. I'm a manager and I ⁶ _____ (+) in an office near my apartment. I ⁷ _____ (+) Mexican food, but I ⁸ _____ (−) Japanese food. In the evenings I ⁹ _____ (+) Spanish at a language school. I ¹⁰ _____ (+) Boston a lot, but it's a very expensive city!

Richard

4B ▷ My free time

Vocabulary free time activities
Grammar Present Simple (*I*, *you*, *we*, *they*):
questions and short answers

QUICK REVIEW Present Simple positive and negative
Write four sentences about you. Use these phrases:
I have … , *I don't have* … , *I live* … , *I work* … , *I like* … ,
I don't like … . Work in pairs. Say your sentences.
Are they the same? A *I have two sisters*. B *Me too*.

Free time activities

1 a Work in pairs. Match these phrases to pictures 1–8.

> go to concerts ☐7 go to the cinema ☐
> go shopping ☐   go out with friends ☐
> play tennis ☐   watch TV or DVDs ☐
> play video games ☐   eat out ☐

b CD2▸5 **PRONUNCIATION** Listen and practise.

2 a Write four sentences about your free time. Use
phrases from **1a**.

I play tennis in my free time.
I watch TV a lot.

b Work in pairs. Say your sentences. Are they the same?

An online interview

3 a Check these words with your teacher.

> a band noise fantastic the weather rap

b CD2▸6 Look at the web page on p33. Read
and listen to the interview with Ruby and Phil
Connor. Find three things they do in their free
time.

4 a Read the interview again. Are these sentences
true (T) or false (F)?

1 Ruby and Phil are married.   *F*
2 They live in a big house in London.
3 They don't like the weather in London.
4 They listen to rock music and rap.
5 They don't watch DVDs.
6 They go to the cinema a lot.
7 They don't like Indian food.
8 They love fruit and chocolate biscuits.

b Work in pairs. Compare answers.

HELP WITH GRAMMAR Present Simple
(*I*, *you*, *we*, *they*): questions and short answers

5 a Look at these questions. Notice the word order.

WH- QUESTIONS (?)

Where	do	you	**live**	in the UK?
What music	do	you	**like**?	

b Write these questions in the table.

1 What **do** you **do** in your free time?
2 What food **do** you **like**?

c Fill in the gaps with *do* or *don't*.

YES / NO QUESTIONS (?)	SHORT ANSWERS
_Do_ you like London?	Yes, I do. No, I _____ .
_____ you go to concerts?	Yes, we _____ . No, we don't.
_____ they like Chinese food?	Yes, they _____ . No, they _____ .

TIP • Present Simple questions are the same for
I, *you*, *we* and *they*.

GRAMMAR 4.2 ▸ p121

Best of British

www.bestofbritish.co.uk/bignoise

HOME   NEWS   INTERVIEWS   TICKETS   PHOTOS   CONCERTS   SHOP

TODAY WE TALK TO RUBY CONNOR AND HER BROTHER, PHIL, FROM THE BRITISH ROCK BAND BIG NOISE.

HI, RUBY AND PHIL. WHERE DO YOU LIVE IN THE UK?
RUBY We have a big flat in Camden, in London.

DO YOU LIKE LONDON?
RUBY Yes, I do. It's a fantastic city and the people are very friendly.
PHIL Yes, I love London too – but we don't like the weather here very much!

WHAT MUSIC DO YOU LIKE?
PHIL We listen to a lot of rock music, of course. We like the Red Hot Chili Peppers, Green Day and Muse.
RUBY We also like rap – we love Eminem and Jay-Z.

WHAT DO YOU DO IN YOUR FREE TIME?
RUBY We go out with friends a lot when we're in London.
PHIL And we watch a lot of DVDs, but we don't go to the cinema.

DO YOU GO TO CONCERTS?
RUBY Yes, we do. A lot of our friends are in bands and we go to their concerts when we have time.

AND THE LAST QUESTION. WHAT FOOD DO YOU LIKE?
PHIL Well, we eat out a lot. We like Indian and Chinese food.
RUBY Yes, and we eat a lot of fruit when we're at home.
PHIL Oh, and we love chocolate biscuits!

THANKS, RUBY AND PHIL. HAVE A NICE DAY!

Big Noise

---

6   a   Fill in the gaps with *do* and these verbs.

~~live~~	do	like (x2)
have	eat	go (x2)

1 Where _do_ Ruby and Phil _live_ ?
2 _____ they _____ a small flat?
3 _____ they _____ the weather in London?
4 What _____ they _____ in their free time?
5 _____ they _____ out with friends a lot?
6 _____ they _____ to the cinema?
7 _____ they _____ Indian food?
8 _____ they _____ a lot of fruit?

b   Work in pairs. Ask and answer the questions.

HELP WITH LISTENING
Questions with *do you*

7   a   CD2 ▶7   Listen to these questions. Notice how we say *do you*.

1 Where do you /dəjə/ live?
2 What music do you /dəjə/ like?
3 Do you /dəjə/ go to concerts?
4 Do you /dəjə/ like Mexican food?

b   CD2 ▶8   Listen and write four questions with *do you*. You will hear each question twice.

c   Work in pairs. Compare questions. Are they the same?

8   a   CD2 ▶9   **PRONUNCIATION**   Listen and practise the questions in **7a** and **7b** and the short answers.

b   Work in pairs. Student A, ask the questions in **7a**. Student B, ask the questions in **7b**. Answer for you.

Get ready … Get it right!

9   Work in new pairs. Student A p86. Student B p91.

▶ REAL WORLD
4C Buying things

Vocabulary things to buy;
this, that, these, those
Real World in a shop

QUICK REVIEW Present Simple Work in pairs. Ask questions with *Do you ...?* and find three things you both do in your free time: **A** *Do you play tennis?* **B** *Yes, I do. / No, I don't.*

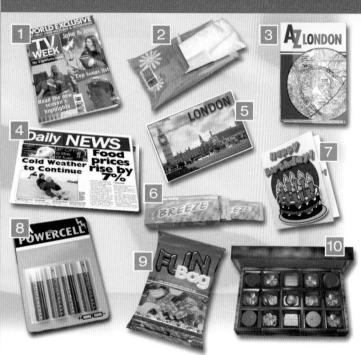

How much is **this** map?

How much are **these** birthday cards?

How much is **that** big box of chocolates?

How much are **those** batteries?

Things to buy

1 a Work in pairs. Match these words to pictures 1–10.

> a magazine [1]   a newspaper [ ]   a map [ ]
> a postcard [ ]   a birthday card [ ]
> a box of chocolates [ ]   tissues [ ]
> sweets [ ]   batteries [ ]   chewing gum [ ]

b CD2 ▶10 PRONUNCIATION Listen and practise.

c Look again at the pictures. Test your partner.

> What's number 1?   A magazine.

HELP WITH VOCABULARY
this, that, these, those

2 Look at photos A–D. Then fill in the table with the words in bold in the questions.

	here ↓	there →
singular		
plural		

VOCABULARY 4.4 ▶ p120

3 CD2 ▶11 PRONUNCIATION Listen and practise the questions in photos A–D.

this → this map → How much is this map?

4 Fill in the gaps with *this*, *that*, *these* or *those*.

1 Are _____ your postcards?

2 _____'s my car!

3 What are _____?

4 Is _____ your newspaper?

Anything else?

5 **a** VIDEO▶4 CD2▶12 Close your books. Then watch or listen to two conversations in a shop. What do the customers buy?

b Watch or listen again. Write the prices in these conversations.

CUSTOMER 1 Excuse me. Do you have any maps of London?
ASSISTANT Yes, they're over there.
C1 Oh, yes. Thanks. How much is this map?
A It's ¹£_____ .
C1 OK. And how much are those batteries?
A They're ²£_____ .
C1 OK. This map and those batteries, please.
A Anything else?
C1 Yes, these sweets, please.
A OK. That's ³£_____ , please.
C1 Here you are.
A Thanks a lot. Goodbye.
C1 Goodbye.

CUSTOMER 2 Hi. How much are these birthday cards?
A They're ⁴£_____ each.
C2 OK, thanks. How much is that big box of chocolates?
A It's ⁵£_____ .
C2 OK. Can I have that box of chocolates and these cards, please?
A Sure. Anything else?
C2 No, that's all, thanks.
A OK. That's ⁶£_____ , please.
C2 Here you are.
A Thanks very much. Goodbye.
C2 Bye.

REAL WORLD In a shop

6 **a** Read these conversations. Fill in the gaps with these words.

~~Excuse~~ much all are lot else have

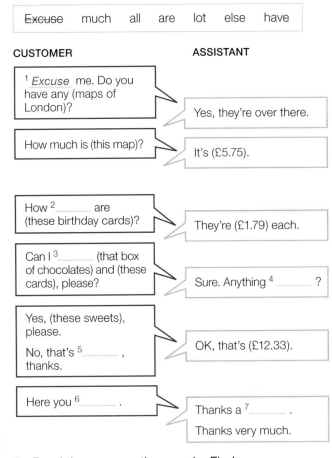

CUSTOMER	ASSISTANT
¹ *Excuse* me. Do you have any (maps of London)?	Yes, they're over there.
How much is (this map)?	It's (£5.75).
How ²_____ are (these birthday cards)?	They're (£1.79) each.
Can I ³_____ (that box of chocolates) and (these cards), please?	Sure. Anything ⁴_____ ?
Yes, (these sweets), please. No, that's ⁵_____ , thanks.	OK, that's (£12.33).
Here you ⁶_____ .	Thanks a ⁷_____ . Thanks very much.

b Read the conversations again. Find:

1 one question with *Do you have …* .
2 one question with *Can I have …* .
3 two questions with *How much …* .

REAL WORLD 4.1 ▶ p121

7 CD2▶13 PRONUNCIATION Listen and practise the sentences in **6a**.

8 Work in pairs. Practise the conversations in **5b**. Take turns to be the customer.

9 Work in the same pairs. Student A p88. Student B p93.

10 **a** Work in new pairs. Write a conversation in a shop. Use language from **1a** and **6a**.

b Practise the conversation until you can remember it.

c Work in groups of four. Role-play your conversation for the other pair. What does the customer buy? How much does he or she spend?

VOCABULARY 4D AND SKILLS

What time is it?

Vocabulary days of the week; time words
Real World telling the time; talking about the time
Skills Reading & Listening: days and times

QUICK REVIEW Things to buy Write ten things you can buy in a shop. Work in pairs. Say the things on your list to your partner. How many are the same?

1 **a** CD2 ▶14 **PRONUNCIATION** Listen and practise the days of the week.

Monday Tuesday
Wednesday Thursday Friday
Saturday Sunday

b Work in pairs. Say a day. Your partner says the next two days.

> Friday

> Saturday, Sunday

c Answer these questions.

1 What day is it **today**?

2 What day is it **tomorrow**?

3 What days are **the weekend**?

2 **a** Put these time words in order.

> a second ☐1 a year ☐7 an hour ☐ a day ☐
> a month ☐ a minute ☐ a week ☐

b CD2 ▶15 **PRONUNCIATION** Listen and check. Listen again and practise.

c Fill in the gaps with words in **2a**. Use the singular or plural.

a 60 _seconds_ = 1 minute

b 60 _____ = 1 hour

c 24 _____ = 1 day

d 7 days = 1 _____

e 365 days = 1 _____

f 12 _____ = 1 year

3 **a** Work in pairs. Match these times to clocks A–D.

> half past six ☐C quarter to seven ☐
> quarter past six ☐ six o'clock ☐

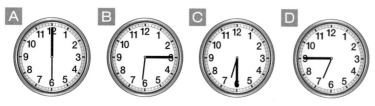

b We can say times in a different way. Work with your partner. Match these times to clocks A–D.

> six ☐A six thirty ☐ six forty-five ☐ six fifteen ☐

4 Match times 1–8 to clocks a–h.

1 five past six _c_
2 ten past six
3 twenty past six
4 twenty-five past six
5 twenty-five to seven
6 twenty to seven
7 ten to seven
8 five to seven

 06:10
 06:50
 06:25
 06:40
 06:05
 06:35
 06:55
 06:20

5 CD2 ▶16 **PRONUNCIATION** Listen and practise the times in **3a** and **4**.

6 **a** CD2 ▶17 Listen and write five times.

b Work in pairs. Compare answers.

7 **a** Look at pictures 1 and 2. Fill in the gaps with these words.

> ~~What~~ half it to time

1 Excuse me. _What_ time is _____, please?

It's twenty _____ three.

2 What _____ is your English class?

It's at _____ past eight.

b CD2 ▶18 **PRONUNCIATION** Listen and check. Listen again and practise.

8 Work in pairs. Student A p89. Student B p94.

9　**a** Check these words with your teacher.

> Europe　unlucky　a flight　an election

b Read about days and times around the world. Choose the correct answers.

DAYS AND TIMES

- In Europe the weekend is ^a*Monday and Tuesday / (Saturday and Sunday)*, but in Egypt and Libya the weekend is ^b*Friday and Saturday / Sunday and Monday.*

- In the USA, children between two and five years old watch TV for ^c*23 / 32* hours a week.

- When it's midday in the UK, it's ^d*morning / afternoon* in Brazil and ^e*morning / afternoon* in China.

- In English-speaking countries ^f*Tuesday 13th/ Friday 13th* is an unlucky day, but in a lot of Spanish-speaking countries ^g*Tuesday 13th/ Friday 13th* is unlucky.

- The flight from Paris to New York is about ^h*7 hours / 11½ hours* and the flight from Bangkok to London is about ⁱ*7 hours / 11½ hours.*

- Elections in Germany, Russia, Poland and Mexico are on ^j*Fridays / Sundays.* Elections in the USA are on ^k*Tuesdays / Thursdays* and in the UK they're on ^l*Tuesdays / Thursdays.*

c Work in pairs. Compare answers.

d　CD2 ▶ 19 Listen and check. How many are correct?

HELP WITH PRONUNCIATION /θ/ and /ð/

1　CD2 ▶ 20 Look at the pictures. Listen to the sounds and words. Listen again and practise.

 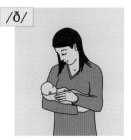

/θ/	/ð/
three	**mo**ther

2　CD2 ▶ 21 Listen to these words. Notice how we say *th* in these words. Listen again and practise.

/θ/	/ð/
three　**th**irteen	**mo**ther　**fa**ther　**bro**ther
thirty　**mon**th	**th**is　**th**at　**th**ese
think　**th**ing　**th**anks	**th**ose　**th**e　**th**en
birthday　**Th**ursday	**th**ey　**wi**th　**th**eir

3　**a**　CD2 ▶ 22 Listen to these sentences. Listen again and practise.

1 I **th**ink **th**at's your mo**th**er.
2 Are **th**ose your **th**ings?
3 It's **th**eir bro**th**er's bir**th**day on **Th**ursday.
4 I **th**ink **th**at man's **th**irty-**th**ree.
5 **Th**anks for **th**ose **th**irteen emails.
6 **Th**is is **th**e first **Th**ursday of **th**e mon**th**.

b Work in pairs. Practise the sentences.

continue2learn

▶ **Vocabulary, Grammar and Real World**

- Extra Practice 4 and Progress Portfolio 4 p100
- **Language Summary 4** p120
- **4A–D** Workbook p18
- **Self-study DVD-ROM 4** with Review Video

▶ **Reading and Writing**

- **Portfolio 4** Internet profiles　Workbook p58
  Reading two internet profiles
  Writing word order (1) & (2); your internet profile

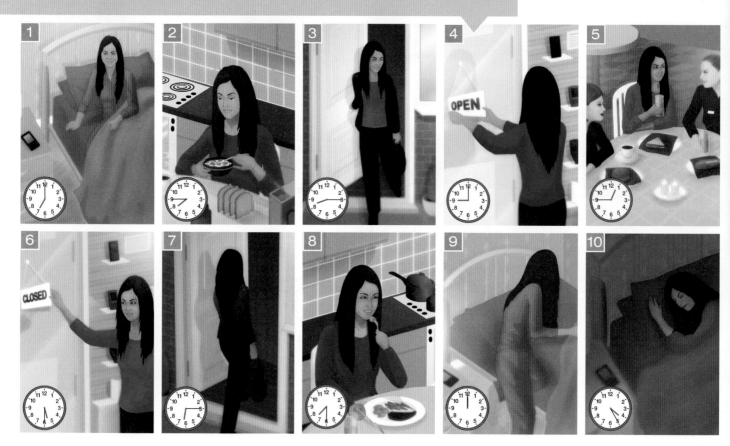

Daily routines

1 a Look at the pictures of Carol's daily routine. Then match these words or phrases to pictures 1–10.

> get up [1]   go to bed [ ]   leave home [ ]
> get home [ ]   start work [ ]   finish work [ ]
> have breakfast [ ]   have lunch [ ]
> have dinner [ ]   sleep [ ]

b CD2 ▷ 23 **PRONUNCIATION** Listen and practise.

c Work in pairs. Match the words and phrases in **1a** to these times of day.

morning	*get up*
afternoon	
evening	
night	

2 a Work in new pairs. Tell your partner what time you do the things in **1a** in the week. What do you do at the same time?

> I get up at seven o'clock.

> Me too!

> I go to bed at eleven.

> I go to bed at half past ten.

b Tell the class things you and your partner do at the same time.

> Magda and I get up at seven o'clock.

Carol's routine

3 a Check these words with your teacher.

> university   midday   midnight   before (10.30)
> after (10.30)   about (10.30)

b Look again at pictures 1–10. Then read about Carol's routine on p39 and fill in the gaps with the correct times.

c CD2 ▷ 24 Listen and check your answers.

Carol and her brother Tom live in Manchester. Carol gets up at ª *7.00* , but she doesn't like mornings! She **has** breakfast at about ᵇ_____ and she **leaves** home at ᶜ_____ . She **works** in a mobile phone shop and she starts work at ᵈ_____ . She has lunch at ᵉ_____ in a café near the shop. She **finishes** work at ᶠ_____ and **gets** home at ᵍ_____ . She has dinner at ʰ_____ . She doesn't watch TV after dinner, she goes out with friends. She **goes** to bed at midnight and **sleeps** for about seven hours.

Carol

HELP WITH GRAMMAR Present Simple (*he*, *she*, *it*): positive and negative

4 **a** Look at these sentences. The verbs in blue are in the Present Simple. Then complete the rule.

POSITIVE (+)

Carol leaves home at 8.15.   She finishes work at 5.30.
She starts work at 9.00.   She gets home at 6.15.

• In positive sentences with *he*, *she* and *it* we add **-s** or _____ to the verb.

b Look at these spelling rules. Fill in the gaps with the verbs in bold in the text about Carol.

spelling rule	examples
most verbs: add -s	likes *leaves* _____ _____
verbs ending in -*ch* or -*sh*: add -es	watches teaches _____
verbs ending in consonant + *y*: *y* → -*ies*	studies _____
the verbs *go* and *do*: add -*es*	_____ does
the verb *have* is irregular	_____

c Look at these sentences. Notice the word order.

NEGATIVE (–)

| She | doesn't | like | mornings. |
| She | doesn't | watch | TV after dinner. |

(doesn't = does not)

TIP • The Present Simple negative is the same for *he*, *she*, *it*: **He** *doesn't have a car.* **It** *doesn't start today.*

GRAMMAR 5.1 ▶ p123

---

5 CD2 ▶ 25 PRONUNCIATION Listen and practise the sentences in **4a** and **4c**.

6 **a** What are the *he*, *she*, *it* forms of these verbs?

1	like	*likes*	5	have		9	eat
2	play		6	study		10	watch
3	start		7	love		11	drink
4	finish		8	go		12	read

b CD2 ▶ 26 PRONUNCIATION Listen and practise. Which *he*, *she*, *it* forms have the sound /ɪz/ at the end?

Tom's routine

7 **a** Read about Carol's brother, Tom. Put the verbs in brackets ( ) in the correct form of the Present Simple.

Tom

Tom's a waiter and he ¹ *works* (work) in a restaurant in the centre of Manchester. He ²_____ (not work) in the morning, so he ³_____ (get up) at midday. He ⁴_____ (not have) breakfast, but he ⁵_____ (have) a big lunch before he ⁶_____ (go) to work. He ⁷_____ (leave) home at 4.30 and he ⁸_____ (start) work at 5.00. He ⁹_____ (finish) work at midnight, but he ¹⁰_____ (not eat) in the restaurant. He ¹¹_____ (have) dinner when he ¹²_____ (get) home and then he ¹³_____ (watch) TV. Tom and Carol ¹⁴_____ (not work) on Mondays, so they ¹⁵_____ (have) lunch together and ¹⁶_____ (talk) about the week.

b CD2 ▶ 27 Listen and check. What do Carol and Tom do on Monday?

Get ready … Get it right!

8 Work in new pairs. Student A p89. Student B p94.

5B ▶ **Where does she work?**

Vocabulary time phrases with *on*, *in*, *at*
Grammar Present Simple (*he*, *she*, *it*):
questions and short answers

QUICK REVIEW Daily routines Work in pairs. Tell each other about your routine in the week: **A** *I get up at six o'clock in the week.* **B** *Really? I get up at about ten!*

Time phrases with *on*, *in*, *at*

1 **a** Write these words and phrases in the correct column.

~~Sunday~~   ~~the morning~~   ~~six o'clock~~   the afternoon
Monday   the evening   Tuesday morning   half past ten
midday   Friday afternoon   midnight   the week
night   the weekend   Saturday evening

on
Sunday

in
the morning

at
six o'clock

b **CD2 ▶ 28** **PRONUNCIATION**
Listen and practise.

2 **a** Fill in the gaps with the correct prepositions.

1 I get up *at* ten o'clock _____ the weekend.
2 Kim goes to bed _____ ten thirty _____ the week.
3 My wife and I go shopping _____ Saturday.
4 Andy has dinner _____ eight o'clock _____ Sunday.
5 We watch TV _____ the evening.
6 My father plays tennis _____ Saturday afternoon.
7 Gary works _____ night and he gets home _____ seven thirty _____ the morning.
8 We play football _____ ten o'clock _____ Sunday morning.

b Write four sentences about you and your family. Use time phrases with *on*, *in*, *at*.

c Work in pairs. Take turns to say your sentences.

Lunch on Monday

3 **a** **CD2 ▶ 29** Look at the photo of Carol, Tom and Nadine. Then listen to their conversation. Choose the correct words in these sentences.

1 Carol has *an espresso* / *a cappuccino*.
2 Nadine *works* / *doesn't work* with Tom.
3 She studies English and *Italian* / *French*.
4 She's from *France* / *Germany*.
5 She lives with *two* / *three* other people.

b Listen again. Answer these questions.

1 Does Tom know Nadine?
   No, he doesn't.
2 Where does Nadine work at the weekend?
3 What does she do in the week?
4 Where does she live in Manchester?
5 Does she like Manchester?
6 What does she do in her free time?

c Work in pairs. Compare answers.

Nadine

Carol

Tom

HELP WITH GRAMMAR Present Simple
(*he*, *she*, *it*): questions and short answers

4 **a** Look at these questions. Notice the word order.

WH- QUESTIONS (?)

Where	does	Nadine	**work**	at the weekend?
What	does	she	**do**	in the week?

TIP • Present Simple questions are the same for *he*, *she* and *it*.

b Write these questions in the table.

1 Where **does** she **live** in Manchester?

2 What **does** she **do** in her free time?

c Fill in the gaps with *does* or *doesn't*.

YES / NO QUESTIONS (?)	SHORT ANSWERS
Does he know Nadine?	Yes, he _____ . No, he doesn't.
_____ she like Manchester?	Yes, she does. No, she _____ .

d Fill in the gaps in these rules with *do* or *does*.

● We use _____ in questions with *he*, *she* and *it*.

● We use _____ in questions with *I*, *you*, *we* and *they*.

GRAMMAR 5.2 ▶ p123

5 **CD2 ▶ 30** **PRONUNCIATION** Listen and practise the questions and short answers in **4**.

HELP WITH LISTENING Sentence stress (1)

6 **a** **CD2 ▶ 31** Listen to these questions. Notice the sentence stress. We stress the important words.

Where does Tom live?

Does he work with Nadine?

Does Nadine like Manchester?

What does she do in the week?

Does she go to the cinema a lot?

What does Tom do?

b Listen again. Is *does* stressed in questions?

7 **a** **CD2 ▶ 31** **PRONUNCIATION** Listen again and practise.

b Work in pairs. Ask and answer the questions in **6a**.

> Where does Tom live?

> In Manchester.

8 Work in the same pairs. Student A p89. Student B p94.

Get ready … Get it right!

9 **a** Work in new pairs. Tell your partner your best friend's name. Is your friend male or female?

b Work on your own. Write five questions with *does* to ask your partner about his or her best friend. Use these ideas or your own.

live   work   study
food and drink
daily routine
free time activities
things he / she likes
things he / she has

Where does Cecilia live?
Does she study English?
What food does she like?

10 **a** Work with your partner from **9a**. Ask and answer your questions. Ask more questions if possible.

> Where does Cecilia live?

> She lives in Lima, in Peru.

b Tell the class two things about your partner's best friend.

What's on the menu?

1 **a** Work in pairs. Look at the restaurant menu. Match photos 1–10 to the food and drink on the menu.

b **CD2 ▶ 32** **PRONUNCIATION** Listen and practise.

2 Work in new pairs. Take turns to choose food and drink from the menu. Ask your partner the price.

> How much is a chicken salad and an orange juice?

> Nine pounds seventy-five.

Are you ready to order?

3 **a** **VIDEO ▶ 5** **CD2 ▶ 33** Martin and Louise are in The Sunrise Restaurant. Watch or listen to their conversation with the waiter. Tick (✓) the food and drink they order on the menu.

b Work in pairs. Compare answers. How much is the bill?

Martin   *Louise*

The SUNRISE Restaurant

MAIN COURSES

chicken salad	£7.25
vegetable lasagne	£7.95
burger and chips	£6.85
mushroom pizza	£7.45

DESSERTS

apple pie and cream	£3.95
fruit salad	£3.50
chocolate, strawberry or vanilla ice cream	£3.25

DRINKS

bottle of mineral water (still or sparkling)	£3.25
orange juice	£2.50
coffee	£2.25
tea	£1.95

REAL WORLD In a restaurant

4 **a** VIDEO 5 CD2 33 Watch or listen again. Tick the customers' sentences when you hear them.

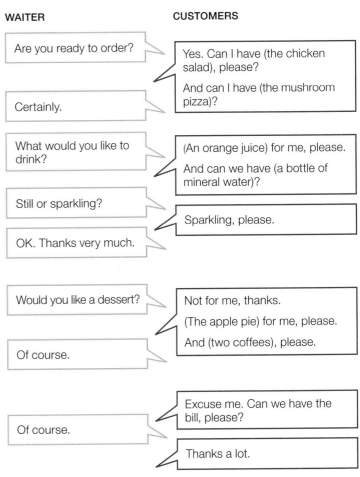

WAITER	CUSTOMERS
Are you ready to order?	Yes. Can I have (the chicken salad), please?
	And can I have (the mushroom pizza)?
Certainly.	
What would you like to drink?	(An orange juice) for me, please.
	And can we have (a bottle of mineral water)?
Still or sparkling?	Sparkling, please.
OK. Thanks very much.	
Would you like a dessert?	Not for me, thanks.
	(The apple pie) for me, please.
	And (two coffees), please.
Of course.	
	Excuse me. Can we have the bill, please?
Of course.	
	Thanks a lot.

b Read the conversations again. Find:

1 two questions with *can I have … .*

2 two questions with *can we have … .*

3 two questions with *would you like … .*

REAL WORLD 5.1 **p123**

5 **a** CD2 34 PRONUNCIATION Listen and practise the sentences in **4a**.

b Work in groups of three. Practise the conversations in **4a**. Take turns to be the waiter or waitress.

6 **a** Work in the same groups. Write a conversation between a waiter or a waitress and two customers at The Sunrise Restaurant. Use language from **4a** and food and drink from the menu.

b Practise your conversation until you can remember it.

c Role-play your conversation for the class. Listen to other groups' conversations. What do they order?

VOCABULARY
5D AND SKILLS ▶ A day off

Vocabulary frequency adverbs and phrases with *every*
Skills Reading and Listening: our Sunday routines; Listening: I love Sundays

QUICK REVIEW Food and drink (3) Work in pairs. Write all the food and drink on the menu at The Sunrise Restaurant. Check your list with another pair. Then check on the menu on p42.

1 **a** Look at these frequency adverbs. Fill in the gaps with *sometimes*, *usually* and *not usually*.

always ———————————————————— never
100% ▮▮▮▮▮▮▮▮▮▮▮▮▮▮▮▮▮▮▮▮▮ 0%

b Put these phrases with *every* in order.

every day 1   every year ☐   every month ☐   every week ☐

c What other time words or phrases do we use with *every*?

every morning   *every Sunday*

d CD2 ▶35 **PRONUNCIATION** Listen and practise.

> I always get up early on Sundays. I never have breakfast because I play football every Sunday morning. I get home at about half past twelve and then I have a big lunch. I don't usually go out in the afternoon, I usually watch sport on TV or read the paper. Then I sometimes sleep for an hour or two. And Becky and I have dinner together at the same restaurant every Sunday evening. Yes, I love my Sunday routine!

Ian

> I'm always tired on Sundays because I work in a hotel every Saturday. So on Sunday mornings I always have breakfast in bed and I never get up before midday! And in the afternoon I usually phone my sister, Amy. She lives in San Francisco, in the USA. And in the evening Ian and I always have dinner at a restaurant called The Sunrise. It's not usually very busy on Sundays and the food there is fantastic!

Becky

2 **a** Check these words with your teacher.

early	late	tired
busy	together	

b CD2 ▶36 Read and listen to Ian and Becky's Sunday routines. What do they always do together on Sundays?

3 **a** Read about Ian and Becky again. Tick (✓) the true sentences. Correct the wrong sentences.

     never
1 Ian ~~always~~ has breakfast on Sundays.
2 He plays football on Sunday mornings. ✓
3 He gets home at about 1.30.
4 He doesn't usually go out in the afternoon.
5 He always sleeps for an hour or two.
6 Becky works in a hotel every Sunday.
7 She has breakfast in bed every Sunday.
8 Her sister lives in the UK.
9 The Sunrise Restaurant is always very busy on Sundays.

b Work in pairs. Compare answers.

HELP WITH VOCABULARY
Frequency adverbs and phrases with *every*

4 Read these rules and the examples.

● **Frequency adverbs** go after *be*:
I**'m always** tired on Sundays.
It**'s not usually** very busy.

● **Frequency adverbs** go before other **verbs**:
I **never have** breakfast.
I **usually watch** sport on TV.

● **Phrases with *every*** are usually at the end of the sentence:
I work in a hotel **every Saturday**.
I play football **every Sunday morning**.

TIP • We can say: *I'm always tired on Sunday / Sundays*.

VOCABULARY 5.4 ▶ p122

5 **a** Make sentences with these words.

1 usually / o'clock / I / at / get up / seven .
I usually get up at seven o'clock.

2 at / eat out / the weekend / sometimes / I .

3 very / 'm / week / always / the / I / in / busy .

4 on / I / Saturdays / usually / work / don't .

5 get up / never / I / the weekend / early / at .

6 tired / I / on / usually / 'm / Mondays .

b Work in pairs. Compare answers. Which sentences are true for you?

Amy · Bruce

6 **a** **CD2 37** Look at the photo of Becky's sister, Amy, and her friend Bruce. Then listen to their conversation about Amy's Sunday routine. Tick (✓) the things they talk about.

- breakfast
- homework
- a concert
- shopping
- children
- DVDs
- phone calls
- lunch
- dinner

b Listen again. Choose the correct answers.

1 Amy always gets up at ⑦ / 8 o'clock on Sundays.

2 She has breakfast with her *husband / friends*.

3 They always have eggs, orange juice and *tea / coffee*.

4 Amy usually talks to Becky for *30 / 60* minutes.

5 Amy has a Spanish class on *Tuesdays / Thursdays*.

6 Amy and Lucas usually have lunch with *Amy's / Lucas's* parents.

HELP WITH LISTENING Sentence stress (2)

7 **a** **CD2 38** Read and listen to these sentences. Notice the stress. We stress the important words.

I always have breakfast with my husband, Lucas.
Yes, I go to a class every Thursday evening.
And we usually go to Lucas's parents for lunch.
And we watch a DVD every Sunday evening.

b Look at Audio Script **CD2 37** p110. Listen to the conversation again. Follow the sentence stress.

8 **a** Write two true sentences and two false sentences about your Sunday routine.

b Work in pairs. Take turns to say your sentences. Guess if your partner's sentences are true or false.

HELP WITH PRONUNCIATION /w/ and /v/

1 **CD2 39** Look at the pictures. Listen to the sounds and words. Listen again and practise.

/w/	/v/

waiter	vegetables

2 **CD2 40** Listen to these words. Notice how we say *w* and *v* in these words. Listen again and practise.

/w/			/v/		
waiter	al**w**ays		**v**egetables	**v**ery	
women	**w**hen	**w**ork	e**v**ening	ne**v**er	li**v**e
where	**W**ednesday		e**v**ery	**v**ocabulary	
week	**w**eekend	t**w**elve	fi**v**e	se**v**en	ele**v**en

3 **a** **CD2 41** Listen to the conversation. Listen again and practise.

A Where do you work?

B I'm a waiter and I work in a very nice café in Vienna.

A When do you work?

B I work every evening from five to eleven in the week.

A Do you work at the weekend?

B Yes, I work seven days a week.

b Work in pairs. Practise the conversation.

---

continue2learn

▶ **Vocabulary, Grammar and Real World**

- Extra Practice 5 and Progress Portfolio 5 p101
- **Language Summary 5** p122
- **5A–D** Workbook p23
- **Self-study DVD-ROM 5** with Review Video

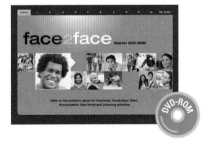

▶ **Reading and Writing**

- **Portfolio 5** My best friend Workbook p60
  Reading best friends
  Writing *because* and *also*; my best friend

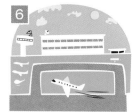

Places in a town or city (1)

1 **a** Match these words to pictures 1–9.

> a building 4   a museum ☐   a theatre ☐
> a shopping centre ☐   a park ☐   a river ☐
> a station ☐   a bus station ☐   an airport ☐

b CD2 ▶43 **PRONUNCIATION** Listen and practise.

c Work in pairs. Cover **1a**. Then test your partner.

> What's number 2?   It's a station.

My city

2 **a** Check these words with your teacher.

> famous   great   hot springs
> swim   a train   a mile

b Look at the photos of Bath, a city in England. What can you see in the photos?

3 **a** CD2 ▶44 Read and listen to Susan. Does she like living in Bath?

b Read about Bath again. Tick (✓) the true sentences. Correct the false sentences.

1 Bath is in ~~the USA~~. *England*
2 It's a very beautiful city. ✓
3 Susan goes to the Thermae Bath Spa every Friday.
4 There are five theatres in Bath.
5 The Jane Austen Centre is a theatre.
6 SouthGate is a big shopping centre.
7 There are trains to London every 15 minutes.
8 Bath doesn't have an airport.

I live in Bath, a city in England. It's a very beautiful place. There are a lot of old buildings in the centre and there are some very nice parks. Bath is famous for its hot springs, and you can swim in the hot water at the Thermae Bath Spa. I go there every Sunday, it's great! In the centre of Bath there are five theatres and some very good museums, including the Roman Baths and the Jane Austen Centre, about the famous English writer. There are also a lot of good restaurants and hotels, and there's a big new shopping centre called SouthGate. There are trains to London every half an hour, and there's an airport in Bristol, only 15 miles away. I think Bath is a great place to live.

Susan

a, some, a lot of; *there is / there are*: positive

4 **a** Match sentences 1–3 to pictures A–C.

1 There's **a person** in the park.
2 There are **some people** in the park.
3 There are **a lot of people** in the park.

b Fill in the gaps with *'s* (= *is*) or *are*.

POSITIVE (+)

SINGULAR	There _____ **a** big new shopping centre.
	There _____ **an** airport in Bristol.
PLURAL	There _____ **five** theatres.
	There _____ **some** very nice parks.
	There _____ **a lot of** old buildings.

`GRAMMAR 6.1` ▶ p125

5 **a** Look at these sentences about Bath. Fill in the gaps with *'s* or *are*.

1 There _'s_ a beautiful river.
2 There _____ two cinemas.
3 There _____ a bus station.
4 There _____ some hot springs.
5 There _____ a nice café near the station.
6 There _____ two five-star hotels.
7 There _____ a famous restaurant called Sally Lunn's.
8 There _____ a lot of trains to London every day.

b `CD2` ▶45 Listen and check. Notice how we say *there's* and *there are*.

There's /ðeəz/ a beautiful river.
There are /ðeərə/ two cinemas.

c `PRONUNCIATION` Listen again and practise.

6 **a** Choose the correct words.

1 There's (a) / *some* station.
2 There are *a* / *three* parks.
3 There are *a* / *some* good museums.
4 There's *a* / *some* bus station.
5 There are *some* / *a* beautiful buildings.
6 There's *a* / *an* old theatre.
7 There are *an* / *a lot of* very good restaurants.
8 There's *an* / *some* airport.
9 There are *some* / *a* nice hotels.
10 There's *a* / *a lot of* river.

b Work in pairs. Compare answers. Which sentences are true for the town or city you are in now?

Get ready … Get it right!

7 Write sentences about a town or city you know (<u>not</u> the town or city you're in now). Use *there is*, *there are* and words from **1a**.

In … there are a lot of nice cafés.
There are some interesting museums.
There's a new shopping centre.

8 **a** Work in pairs. Tell your partner about your town or city in **7**.

b Tell the class two things about your partner's town or city.

6B   Are there any shops?

Vocabulary places in a town or city (2)
Grammar *there is / there are*: negative,
yes / no questions and short answers; *any*

QUICK REVIEW **there is / there are** Work
in pairs. Say sentences about the town or
city you are in now. Use *there is* and *there
are*: **A** *There are some good restaurants in
the centre.* **B** *Yes, and there's a nice park.*

Places in a town or city (2)

1 a Work in pairs. Match these words to
pictures 1–9.

> a road [3]   a bank ☐   a market ☐
> a chemist's ☐   a post office ☐
> a supermarket ☐   a bus stop ☐
> a square ☐   a cashpoint / an ATM ☐

b CD2 46 **PRONUNCIATION** Listen and
practise.

c Work with your partner. Close your
books. How many places in a town or
city do you remember?

Welcome to my home

2 a CD2 47 Look at the photo of Susan
and her friend, Isabel. Listen to their
conversation. Put these things in the
order they talk about them.

- Susan's flat   *1*
- restaurants
- shops
- trains and buses
- banks

b Listen again. Choose the correct words.

1 Susan (*likes*) / *doesn't like* living in her flat.

2 There are *some* / *a lot of* shops in Susan's
road.

3 There's a cashpoint at the *supermarket* /
post office.

4 It's *a mile* / *two miles* to the centre of Bath.

5 There are buses to the centre of Bath
every *ten* / *twenty* minutes.

6 There's a *station* / *bus stop* near the post
office.

7 There are some very nice restaurants
near Susan's house / *in the centre*.

c Work in pairs. Compare answers.

Susan   Isabel

3 **a** Fill in the gaps with *aren't* or *isn't*.

NEGATIVE (–)

1 There _____ a station near here.

2 There _____ any good restaurants near here.

b Fill in the gaps with *is, are, isn't* or *aren't*.

YES / NO QUESTIONS (?)	SHORT ANSWERS
Is there a bank?	Yes, there _____ . No, there _____ .
_____ there any shops?	Yes, there _____ . No, there _____ .

c Look again at the sentences in **3a** and **3b**. Then choose the correct word in this rule.

● We use *some / any* in negatives and questions with *there are*.

GRAMMAR 6.2 ▶ p125

HELP WITH LISTENING Linking (1)

4 **CD2** ▶ 48 Listen to these sentences. Notice the linking between the **consonant** sounds and the **vowel** sounds.

1 There's_an_expensive market.

2 There_are some_old buildings.

3 There_isn't_an_airport.

4 There_aren't_any museums.

5 Is there_a post_office?

6 Are there_any nice_old cafés?

5 **CD2** ▶ 49 **PRONUNCIATION** Listen and practise the sentences in **4** and the short answers.

There's_an_expensive market.

6 **a** Write sentences about places near Susan's flat.

1 (✓) a supermarket
There's a supermarket.

2 (✗) a shopping centre
There isn't a shopping centre.

3 (✓) a market

4 (✗) any museums

5 (✓) a park

6 (✗) a square

7 (✗) any nice cafés

8 (✓) a lot of old houses

b Work in pairs. Compare answers.

7 Work in the same pairs. Student A p86. Student B p91.

Get ready ... Get it right!

8 Write eight questions to ask another student about places near his or her home. Use the words on the map (a cinema, hotels, etc.), *Is there a ... ?* and *Are there any ... ?*.

Is there a cinema near your home?
Are there any hotels?

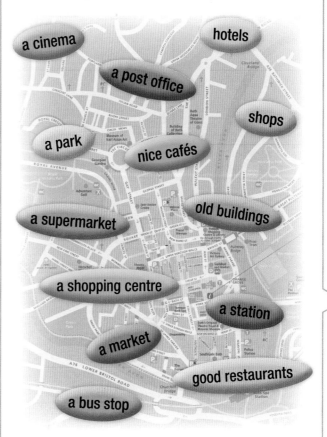

9 **a** Work in pairs. Take turns to ask your questions from **8**. Make notes on your partner's answers. Give more information about places near your home if possible.

| Is there a cinema near your home? | Yes, there is. It's five minutes away. |
| Are there any hotels? | No, there aren't. |

b Work in new pairs. Talk about places near your first partner's home.

There's a cinema near Gabi's home, but there aren't any hotels.

c Tell the class about one interesting place near your partner's home.

QUICK REVIEW Places in a town or city   Write ten words for places in a town or city (a square, etc.). Work in pairs. Compare lists. Which places are near your school?

Things in your bag (2)

1 a Work in pairs. Match these words to things 1–11.

> a wallet 8   a purse ☐   keys ☐   money ☐
> a credit card ☐   a passport ☐   an ID card ☐
> a guide book ☐   a map ☐   a camera ☐
> a laptop ☐

b CD2 ▶50 **PRONUNCIATION** Listen and practise.

c Work in new pairs. Which things in **1a** do you have with you?

> I have some money with me.   Yes, me too.

When is it open?

2 a Check these words with your teacher.

> a tourist   an art gallery   open
> closed   book a walking tour

b VIDEO ▶6 CD2 ▶51 Martin and Louise are at the tourist information centre in Cambridge. Watch or listen to their conversation. Put photos A–C in order.

3 VIDEO ▶6 CD2 ▶51 Watch or listen again. Choose the correct answers.

1 Martin wants a (map) / guide book of Cambridge.
2 Kettle's Yard art gallery is open from 10.30 / 11.30 a.m. to 5 / 6 p.m.
3 The gallery is open / closed on Mondays.
4 The Fitzwilliam Museum is about 5 / 10 minutes away.
5 The walking tours start at 10 / 11 a.m. and 1 / 2 p.m.
6 They are £7.50 / £17.50 per person.

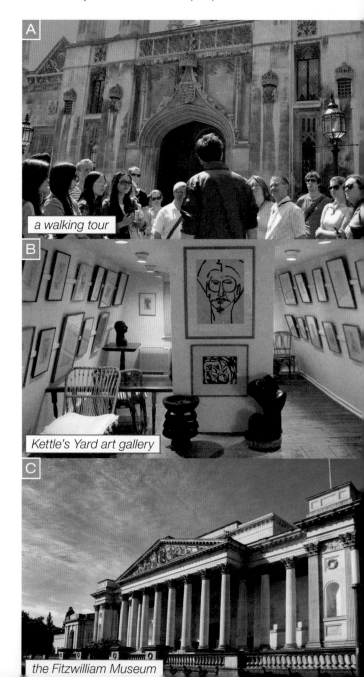

A *a walking tour*

B *Kettle's Yard art gallery*

C *the Fitzwilliam Museum*

Martin   Louise

REAL WORLD At a tourist information centre

4 Read these conversations. Fill in the gaps with these words.

~~help~~   book   have   start   map   closed   open

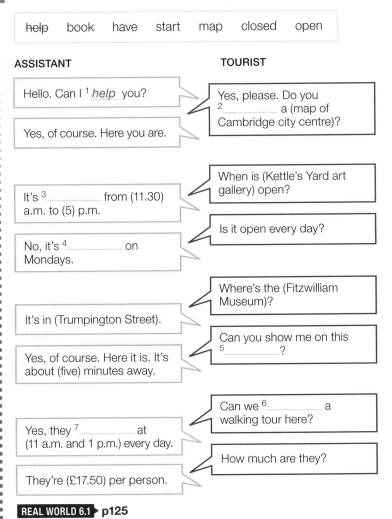

ASSISTANT

Hello. Can I ¹ *help* you?

Yes, of course. Here you are.

It's ³_____ from (11.30) a.m. to (5) p.m.

No, it's ⁴_____ on Mondays.

It's in (Trumpington Street).

Yes, of course. Here it is. It's about (five) minutes away.

Yes, they ⁷_____ at (11 a.m. and 1 p.m.) every day.

They're (£17.50) per person.

TOURIST

Yes, please. Do you ²_____ a (map of Cambridge city centre)?

When is (Kettle's Yard art gallery) open?

Is it open every day?

Where's the (Fitzwilliam Museum)?

Can you show me on this ⁵_____?

Can we ⁶_____ a walking tour here?

How much are they?

REAL WORLD 6.1 ▶ **p125**

5 **a** CD2 ▶ 52 **PRONUNCIATION** Listen and practise the sentences in **4**.

Hello. Can I help you?

b Work in pairs. Practise the conversations in **4**. Take turns to be the tourist.

6 **a** Choose the correct words or phrases in these conversations.

1

ASSISTANT Hello. ¹*I can / Can I* help you?

TOURIST Yes, please. ²*When / Where* is the Sedgwick Museum open?

A It's open today ³*from / to* 10 a.m. ⁴*from / to* 4 p.m.

T ⁵*Is it / Is* open every day?

A No, it's closed ⁶*in / on* Sundays.

T OK, thanks. And ⁷*where's / there's* the ADC Theatre?

A It's ⁸*in / at* Park Street.

T Can you show me on this ⁹*card / map*?

A Yes, of course. ¹⁰*Here is it. / Here it is.* It's about ten minutes away.

2

T Good ¹¹*afternoon / night*. Do you have a map ¹²*in / of* the UK?

A Yes, ¹³*here you are / here are you*.

T Thank you. And can I ¹⁴*make / book* a bus tour here?

A Yes, they start ¹⁵*at / on* 10 a.m. and 2 p.m. every ¹⁶*day / days*.

T How much ¹⁷*is / are* they?

A They're £17.50 per ¹⁸*person / people*.

T OK. Thanks a lot. Goodbye.

b CD2 ▶ 53 Listen and check.

c Work in pairs. Practise the conversations in **6a**. Take turns to be the tourist.

7 **a** Work in new pairs. Imagine you are in a tourist information centre in the town or city you are in now. Write a conversation between a tourist and an assistant. Use language from **4** and your own ideas.

b Practise your conversation until you can remember it.

c Work in groups of four with another pair. Take turns to role-play your conversations. What does the tourist ask about?

VOCABULARY
6D AND SKILLS > It's my favourite

Vocabulary clothes, colours, *favourite*
Skills Listening: my clothes;
Reading: my favourite places

QUICK REVIEW **Things in your bag** Work in pairs. What things do you both have with you today?
A *Do you have any keys with you?* **B** *Yes, I do.* **A** *Me too.* **B** *Do you have a laptop with you?*

Wayne

Monica

Brad

Lisa

1 **a** Work in pairs. Look at the photos of Wayne, Monica, Brad and Lisa. Match these words to clothes 1–14.

a suit 3	a tie ☐	a shirt ☐	a T-shirt ☐	a jumper ☐
a jacket ☐	a coat ☐	a skirt ☐	a dress ☐	
trousers ☐	jeans ☐	shoes ☐	trainers ☐	boots ☐

b CD2 54 PRONUNCIATION Listen and practise.

c Work in new pairs. Test your partner.

> What's number 1?   It's a shirt.

2 CD2 55 PRONUNCIATION Listen and practise these colours.

black **white** **yellow**
brown **red** **blue**
grey **pink** **green**

3 **a** Look at the photos for two minutes. Remember the people's names, their clothes and the colours.

b Work in pairs. Student A, close your book. Student B, ask what colour the people's clothes are. Then change roles.

> What colour are Monica's boots?   They're black.

4 **a** CD2 56 Look again at the photos. Listen and put the people in the order you hear them.

b Listen again. What does each person never wear?

5 **a** Which clothes and colours do you: usually wear, sometimes wear, never wear? Write three lists.

b Work in groups. Tell other students about the things on your lists.

> I usually wear a T-shirt and jeans.

> I sometimes wear boots.   I never wear pink.

HELP WITH VOCABULARY *favourite*

6 **a** Fill in the gaps with *This, These, My, Who* or *What*.

1 _____ favourite colour is pink.
2 _____ is my favourite jacket.
3 _____ are my favourite boots.
4 _____'s your favourite colour?
5 _____'s your favourite actor?

b CD2 57 PRONUNCIATION Listen and practise.

VOCABULARY 6.6 > p125

7 **a** Read the blog. Fill in the gaps with these words.

clothes shop   café   restaurant

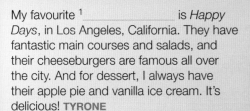

My favourite places

My favourite ¹_____ is *Happy Days*, in Los Angeles, California. They have fantastic main courses and salads, and their cheeseburgers are famous all over the city. And for dessert, I always have their apple pie and vanilla ice cream. It's delicious! **TYRONE**

My favourite ²_____ is called *Francesca's*. It's in Covent Garden market in the centre of London. They sell beautiful dresses, trousers, jackets, jumpers and skirts, and they aren't very expensive. I go shopping there every weekend with my friends. **SUNEE**

My favourite ³_____ is called *The Kangaroo* in Melbourne, Australia. I go there for breakfast every morning on my way to work. It has great coffee, delicious hot croissants and very good sandwiches. The waiters are very friendly and they always play great music. **KEIRA**

b Read the blog again. Answer these questions.

1 Are the cheeseburgers at *Happy Days* famous?
2 What does Tyrone always have for dessert?
3 Are the clothes at Francesca's very expensive?
4 When does Sunee go shopping there?
5 When does Keira go to *The Kangaroo*?
6 Are the waiters very friendly?

8 **a** Write six questions with *your favourite*. Use these ideas or your own.

food   actor   musician   drink
restaurant   actress   band   café
singer   colour   day   sport

What's your favourite food?
Who's your favourite actor?

b Work in pairs. Take turns to ask your questions.

c Tell the class two things about your partner.

HELP WITH PRONUNCIATION /tʃ/ and /dʒ/

1 **CD2** ▶58 Look at the pictures. Listen to the sounds and words. Listen again and practise.

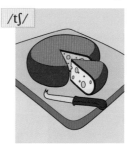
/tʃ/

/dʒ/

cheese   orange juice

2 **CD2** ▶59 Listen to these words. Notice how we say the **pink** and **blue** letters. Listen again and practise.

/tʃ/	/dʒ/
cheese **ch**eap mu**ch**	**or**a**nge** **j**uice **j**eans
chips **ch**o**c**olate **ch**i**ck**en	**j**umper **j**a**ck**et mana**g**er
children pi**c**ture	pa**ge** **j**ob ve**g**etables
sandwi**ch** Fren**ch**	langua**ge** **J**apanese

3 **a** A lot of English first names start with /dʒ/. Work in pairs. How do we say these names?

male 🚹	Jack John James Jim Jason
	Jeremy Joe Justin Geoff George
female 🚺	Jane Jan Jessica Jenny Julia
	Juliet Joanna Jill Gillian Gina

b **CD2** ▶60 Listen and check. Listen again and practise.

continue2learn

▶ **Vocabulary, Grammar and Real World**
- **Extra Practice 6 and Progress Portfolio 6** p102
- **Language Summary 6** p124
- **6A–D** Workbook p28
- **Self-study DVD-ROM 6** with Review Video

▶ **Reading and Writing**
- **Portfolio 6** A tourist in London Workbook p62
  Reading a newspaper article
  Writing describing places; places for tourists in your town or city

QUICK REVIEW Favourite What's your favourite: city, sport, shop, film, book, colour? Work in groups. Tell the other students your favourite things. Are any the same? **A** *My favourite city is Paris.* **B** *Me too.* **C** *My favourite city is Rome.*

Things you like and don't like

1 **a** Work in pairs. Match these words and phrases to pictures 1–9.

> soap operas 7   visiting new places ☐   classical music ☐
> flying ☐   dancing ☐   watching sport on TV ☐   animals ☐
> horror films ☐   shopping for clothes ☐

b CD2 ▶61 **PRONUNCIATION** Listen and practise.

2 Match these phrases to pictures A–D.

> I like …   I hate …   I don't like …   I love …

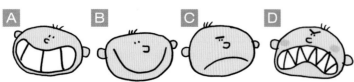

HELP WITH VOCABULARY
love, like, don't like, hate

3 **a** Look at these sentences. After *love, like, don't like* and *hate* we can use a **noun** or **verb+*ing***.

I love **animals**.
I like **soap operas**.
I don't like **dancing**.
I hate **shopping** for clothes.

b Find all the **verb+*ing*** words in **1a**.

c Look at how we make **verb+*ing*** words in VOCABULARY 7.2 ▷ p126.

4 **a** Write the verb+*ing* forms of the verbs in brackets.

1 I love *playing* tennis. (play)
2 I like _____ a sister. (have)
3 I hate _____ to concerts. (go)
4 I don't like _____ early. (get up)
5 I like _____ in the afternoon. (sleep)
6 I love _____ in this town/city. (live)

b Work in pairs. Compare answers. Are any of these sentences true for you?

5 **a** Write three true sentences and three false sentences about things you love, like, don't like and hate. Use words and phrases from **1a** or your own ideas.

I love going to museums.
I don't like soap operas.

b Work in pairs. Say your sentences. Guess if your partner's sentences are true or false.

> I love going to museums.

> I think that's true.

> No, it's false!

We're very different

6 **a** Check these words with your teacher.

> twins   different   similar
> the same   both

b Do you know any twins? If so, tell the class about them (names, age, jobs, family, etc.).

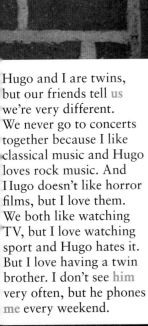

Hugo and I are twins, but our friends tell **us** we're very different. We never go to concerts together because I like classical music and Hugo loves rock music. And Hugo doesn't like horror films, but I love them. We both like watching TV, but I love watching sport and Hugo hates it. But I love having a twin brother. I don't see **him** very often, but he phones **me** every weekend.

Adam

Our mum says Adam and I are very similar, but I don't agree with **her**. Adam and I both like watching TV, but I love soap operas and he hates **them**. We don't often eat out together because I like Mexican food and he loves Japanese food. And I don't like flying, but Adam loves **it**. I know we don't like the same things, but I love having a twin brother!

Hugo

7 **a** [CD2▶62] Read and listen to Adam and Hugo. Find two things they both like.

b Read about Adam and Hugo again. Fill in the gaps in these sentences with *Adam* or *Hugo*.

1 *Adam* likes classical music.
2 _____ likes horror films.
3 _____ hates watching sport on TV.
4 _____ hates soap operas.
5 _____ likes Mexican food.
6 _____ doesn't like flying.
7 _____ phones _____ every weekend.

HELP WITH GRAMMAR Object pronouns

8 **a** Look at these sentences. Notice the word order.

subject	verb	object
I	love	soap operas.
Adam	hates	them.

b Look again at the texts about Adam and Hugo. Fill in the table with the object pronouns in blue.

subject pronouns	I	you	he	she	it	we	they
object pronouns		you					

GRAMMAR 7.1 ▶ p127

9 **a** Fill in the gaps with object pronouns.

1 A Do you like studying English?
  B Yes, I love _it_ .
2 A Do you like Lady Gaga?
  B Yes, I like _____ a lot.
3 A Do you like getting up early?
  B No, I hate _____ .
4 A Do you like Johnny Depp?
  B Yes, I love _____ !
5 A Do you like soap operas?
  B No, I hate _____ .
6 A Do you like dogs?
  B Yes, but they don't like _____ !

b [CD2▶63] [PRONUNCIATION] Listen and check. Listen again and practise.

c Work in pairs. Take turns to ask the questions in 9a. Answer for you.

10 **a** Write five questions about Adam and Hugo with *Does … like … ?*

Does Adam like rock music?

b Work in pairs. Ask and answer the questions.

Get ready … Get it right!

11 Work in new pairs. Student A p86. Student B p91.

QUICK REVIEW **Things you like** Work in pairs.
Ask questions and find four things you both like:
A *Do you like cats?* **B** *Yes, I do. / No, I don't.*
Do you like flying? **A** *Yes, I love it. / No, I hate it.*

Abilities

1 **a** Match these words and phrases to pictures 1–10.

swim 4   cook ☐   drive ☐   ride a bike ☐
play basketball ☐   play the piano ☐   sing ☐
play the guitar ☐   speak German ☐   ski ☐

Guten Tag!

b CD2▶64 **PRONUNCIATION** Listen and practise.

c Work in pairs. Mime activities from **1a**. Guess your partner's activities.

I can't swim!

2 Match sentences 1–4 to pictures A–D.

1 Help! I can't swim!   3 Sorry, we can't speak Chinese.
2 She can play the piano.   4 They can ski very well.

HELP WITH GRAMMAR *can*: positive and negative

3 We use *can* or *can't* to talk about ability. Look at these sentences. Then read the rule.

POSITIVE (+)

She	**can**	play	the piano.
They	**can**	ski.	

NEGATIVE (–)

I	**can't**	swim.	
We	**can't**	speak	Chinese.

● *Can* and *can't* are the same for *I, you, he, she, it, we* and *they*.

TIP • We sometimes use **(very) well** with *can*:
*She can swim **well**. They can ski **very well**.*

GRAMMAR 7.2 ▶ p127

HELP WITH LISTENING *can* or *can't*

4 **a** CD2▶65 Listen to these sentences. Notice how we say *can* and *can't*. Is *can* stressed? Is *can't* stressed?

Help! I can't /kɑːnt/ swim!
She can /kən/ play the piano.
Sorry, we can't /kɑːnt/ speak Chinese.
They can /kən/ ski very well.

b CD2▶66 Listen to six sentences. Do you hear *can* or *can't*?

5 **CD2▶66** **PRONUNCIATION** Listen again and practise.

I can /kən/ play the guitar.

6 **a** Write three true sentences and three false sentences about you and your family. Use *can* or *can't*.

I can't play the piano.
My brother can speak Japanese very well.

b Work in pairs. Say your sentences. Guess if your partner's sentences are true or false.

Help with the children

7 **a** **CD2▶67** Look at the photo. Mrs Taylor wants an au pair to help with her children, Megan and Harry. Listen to the interview. Does Natalia get the job?

b Listen again. Put a tick (✓) for the things Natalia can do. Put a cross (✗) for the things she can't do.

1 cook ✓	6 play tennis
2 drive	7 play football
3 speak German	8 play the piano
4 speak French	9 sing
5 swim	10 play the guitar

c Work in pairs. Compare answers.

HELP WITH GRAMMAR
can: yes / no questions and short answers

8 Look at these questions. Then fill in the gaps in the short answers with *can* or *can't*.

YES / NO QUESTIONS (?)	SHORT ANSWERS
Can you **cook**?	Yes, I *can* . / No, I _____ .
Can he **play** the guitar?	Yes, he _____ . / No, he _____ .
Can she **speak** French?	Yes, she _____ . / No, she _____ .
Can they **swim**?	Yes, they _____ . / No, they _____ .

GRAMMAR 7.3 ▶ p127

9 **CD2▶68** **PRONUNCIATION** Listen and practise the questions and short answers in **8**.

Can /kən/ you cook?   Yes, I can /kæn/.

10 Work in pairs. Student A p90. Student B p95.

Get ready … Get it right!

11 Make a list of things you can do. Use words and phrases from **1a** and your own ideas.

play the guitar

12 **a** Work in new pairs. Ask questions to find things you can both do. Use your list from **11**.

> Can you play the guitar?

> Yes, I can. / No, I can't.

b Tell the class things you can both do.

Mrs Taylor

Natalia

Where's the café?

1 a Write ten places in a town or city.

a restaurant   a café

b Work in groups. Compare lists. Do you have the same places?

HELP WITH VOCABULARY
Prepositions of place

2 Where's the café? Match pictures a–f to sentences 1–6.

1 It's **in** King Street.   *c*
2 It's **near** the bank.
3 It's **next to** the bank.
4 It's **opposite** the bank.
5 It's **on** the left.
6 It's **on** the right.

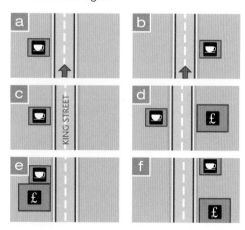

TIP • We can say **in** *King Street* or **on** *King Street*.

VOCABULARY 7.4 ▶ p126

3 a **CD3 ▶ 1** **PRONUNCIATION** Listen and practise the sentences in **2**.

b Work in pairs. Ask where the café is in pictures a–f.

> Where's the café in picture c?

> It's in King Street.

Rachel

Jack

It's over there

4 a Work in new pairs. Look at the map on p59. What are places 1–12?

b Say where a place is on the map. Your partner guesses the place.

> It's in New Road, opposite the park.

> The cinema.

5 a **VIDEO ▶ 7** **CD3 ▶ 2** Look at the photos of Rachel and Jack. They are at ✳ on the map. Then watch or listen. Which places do they want to go to?

b Work in pairs. Look again at the map. Choose the correct words in these conversations.

RACHEL Excuse me. Where's the [1]*museum / station*?
MAN Go along this road and turn left. That's Park Street. The [2]*museum / station* is [3]*on / in* the right, [4]*opposite / next to* the theatre.
R Thanks very much. Oh, and is there a [5]*chemist's / café* near here?
M Yes, there is. Go along this road and it's [6]*at / on* the left, [7]*opposite / next to* the hotel.
R OK. Thanks a lot.
M No problem.

JACK Excuse me. Where's the [8]*theatre / post office*?
WOMAN It's over there, [9]*near / opposite* the cinema.
J Oh, yes. I [10]*can / can't* see it. Thanks.
W You're welcome.
J Also, is there a [11]*supermarket / bank* near here?
W Yes, there's one [12]*in / at* Station Road. Go along this road and turn right. The [13]*supermarket / bank* is on the [14]*left / right*, opposite the station.
J OK, thanks a lot. Bye.

c Watch or listen again. Check your answers.

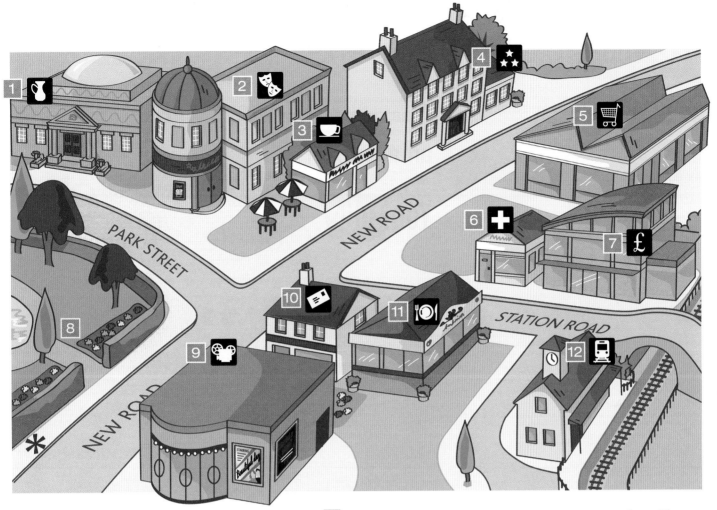

REAL WORLD
Asking for and giving directions

6 Fill in the gaps with these words.

> ~~me~~   to   turn   on   road   here   over

ASKING FOR DIRECTIONS

Excuse ¹ _me_ . Where's the (museum)?
Excuse me. Is there a (bank) near ² _____ ?

GIVING DIRECTIONS

Go along this ³ _____ and turn left.
Go along this road and ⁴ _____ right.
That's (Park Street).
The (museum) is on the right, next ⁵ _____
the (theatre).
The (bank) is ⁶ _____ the left, opposite
the (station).
It's ⁷ _____ there, near the (cinema).

REAL WORLD 7.1 ▸ **p127**

7 **a** **CD3** ▸3 **PRONUNCIATION** Listen and practise
the sentences in **6**.

Excuse me. Where's the museum?

b Work in pairs. Practise the conversations
in **5b**. Take turns to be Rachel and Jack.

8 **a** Look again at the map. Read these conversations. The
people are at ✳ on the map. Choose the correct words.

1

A Excuse ¹*you / me*. Is there a restaurant near ²*here / there*?
B Yes, there is. Go along this road and turn ³*left / right*. That's
Station Road. The restaurant is ⁴*in / on* the right, ⁵*near / in*
the station.
A Thank you very much.

2

A Excuse me. ⁶*Where's / What's* the theatre?
B It's ⁷*near / over* there, ⁸*opposite / next to* the museum.
A Oh yes. I can see it. Thanks a lot.
B You're welcome.

3

A Excuse me. Is there a supermarket ⁹*next to / near* here?
B Yes, there is. Go ¹⁰*to / along* this road. The supermarket is
on the ¹¹*left / right*, opposite the ¹²*hotel / café*.
A Thanks a lot.

b **CD3** ▸4 Listen and check.

c Work in the same pairs. Practise the conversations in **8a**.
Take turns to ask for directions.

9 Work in new pairs. You are at ✳ on the map. Ask for directions
to places on the map. Are your partner's directions correct?

VOCABULARY
7D AND SKILLS ▷ **The internet**

Vocabulary things people do online
Skills Reading: It's my internet!;
Listening: an internet questionnaire

QUICK REVIEW Directions Write five places (cafés, restaurants, shops, etc.) near your school. Work in pairs. Do you know your partner's places? If not, ask for directions.

1 a Work in pairs. Look at these things people do on the internet. Fill in the gaps with these words.

> ~~send~~ watch chat be
> buy read hotels the radio
> music information flights

send
get / receive	emails
sell	things online
write	a blog
	TV programmes
videos
	on Facebook
on Twitter
download	videos
_____
apps
book	holidays
listen	to _____
to music
	to friends and family
search	for _____

TIPS • *online* = connected to the internet
• *a TV programme* (UK) = *a TV show* (US)

b **CD3▶5** **PRONUNCIATION** Listen and practise the phrases in **1a**.

2 Work in new pairs. What can people do on these websites?

> You can book hotels or holidays on lastminute.com.

3 a Read about how three people use the internet. Fill in the gaps with *Sunita*, *Brian* and *Millie*.

1 *Millie* works in a restaurant.
2 _____ checks her Facebook page every day.
3 _____ isn't on Facebook or Twitter.
4 _____ watches TV programmes online.
5 _____ uses the internet for directions.
6 _____ chats to her brother online.
7 _____ writes a blog.
8 _____ doesn't buy things online.
9 _____ and _____ buy clothes online.

● ● ● ◀▷ ● www.howdoyouusetheinternet.com ↻ ⌕ ⌂

It's my internet!

SUNITA How do I use the internet? Well, I'm on Facebook and I check that every day. I also chat online to my brother a lot – he lives in Australia, you see. I download a lot of music onto my laptop and I watch music videos on YouTube. Oh, and I buy a lot of things online – DVDs, shoes, clothes, books. Yes, I can't live without the internet!

BRIAN I don't use the internet very much. I send and receive emails, of course, but I'm not on Facebook or Twitter. And I sometimes use the internet to search for information, for example, directions to a place I don't know. I also book hotels on the internet, but I never buy things online – I like looking at things before I buy them.

MILLIE I use the internet to write a blog about my life. I'm a waitress in Hollywood and a lot of famous people eat in our restaurant. My blog's very popular, but I don't use my real name. I also watch a lot of TV shows online because I don't have a TV. Oh, and I buy a lot of things online too. I love shopping for clothes on eBay!

b Read about the people again. Underline phrases from **1a**. Then compare with another student.

Sam

Internet Questionnaire

A things people do online	B Sam (✓ or ✗)	C your partner (✓ or ✗)
¹watch / listen TV programmes		
²watch / listen to the radio		
³send / be on Facebook		
⁴download / chat to friends and family		
buy and ⁵search / sell things		
⁶chat / book flights or holidays		
⁷read / watch blogs		
⁸book / download music		

4 a Look at column A in the questionnaire. Choose the correct verbs.

b CD3▶6 Look at the photo. Then listen to Sam's interview. Put a tick (✓) or a cross (✗) in column B of the questionnaire.

c Listen again. Answer these questions.

1 Does Sam watch videos online?
2 What's his favourite website?
3 Is he on Twitter?
4 Where does his sister live?
5 What does he buy on Amazon?
6 Is Sam married or single?
7 Where does he listen to music?

5 a Work in pairs. Look again at the questionnaire. Interview your partner. Put a tick (✓) or a cross (✗) in column C. Give more information if possible.

b Work in new pairs. Talk about your partner in **5a**.

c Tell the class two things about your first partner.

HELP WITH PRONUNCIATION /s/ and /ʃ/

1 CD3▶7 Look at the pictures. Listen to the sounds and words. Listen again and practise.

/s/
suit

/ʃ/
shirt

2 CD3▶8 Listen to these words. Notice how we say the **pink** and **blue** consonants. Listen again and practise.

/s/	/ʃ/
suit **s**mall **s**kirt **s**ell **c**entre **c**ity poli**c**e pen**c**il expen**s**ive le**ss**on **S**panish	**sh**irt **sh**e **sh**op **s**ugar ti**ss**ues **s**ure Turki**sh** Briti**sh** Egyptian Ru**ss**ian Spani**sh**

3 a CD3▶9 Listen to this poem. Listen again and practise.

Sharon **S**mith has a **s**mall **sh**op
In **Sh**anghai **c**ity **c**entre
She **s**ells **S**panish **s**kirts and Turki**sh** shirt**s**
And expen**s**ive Briti**sh** **s**uit**s**
She **s**ells Egyptian boot**s** and Ru**ss**ian coat**s**
What can **sh**e **s**ell you?

b Work in pairs. Take turns to say lines of the poem.

▶ continue2learn

▶ Vocabulary, Grammar and Real World
■ **Extra Practice 7 and Progress Portfolio 7** p103
■ **Language Summary 7** p126
■ **7A–D** Workbook p33
■ **Self-study DVD-ROM 7** with Review Video

▶ Reading and Writing
■ **Portfolio 7** The same or different? Workbook p64
Reading people in my family
Writing sentences with *and*, *but* and object pronouns; word order (3); *both* and *together*

8A I was there

Vocabulary adjectives (2)
Grammar Past Simple of *be*:
positive and negative

QUICK REVIEW Things people do online Write six phrases for things people do online (*send emails*, etc.). Work in groups. Compare phrases and say which of the things you do every day or every week. **A** *I send emails every day*.

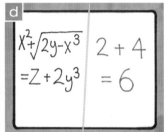

Three amazing days

2 **a** Check these words with your teacher.

> a stadium   a seat   New Year's Eve
> fireworks   a party   a football match

b **CD3** ▶ **11** Read and listen to Melanie, Tania and Diego. What were their 'amazing days'?

c Read the texts again. Choose the correct words in these sentences.

1 The Beatles' last concert was in *the UK / the USA*.
2 The concert was about *an hour / half an hour* long.
3 Tania was in Sydney with her *parents / friends*.
4 The fireworks at midnight were *fantastic / boring*.
5 Diego's friends were from *Spain / Holland*.
6 He was at the match with *two / three* other people.

> I was at the Beatles' last concert.
> It was in San Francisco in 1966.
> There were 25,000 people at the
> concert, but the stadium wasn't
> full – there were about 17,000
> empty seats! The concert wasn't
> very long, only 33 minutes, but
> I was very happy to be there.
> I was only sixteen at the time.

Adjectives (2)

1 **a** Match these adjectives to pictures a–h.

short	*a*	long
happy	☐	unhappy
interesting	☐	boring
full	☐	empty
difficult	☐	easy
right	☐	wrong
old	☐	young
terrible, awful	☐	great, fantastic, amazing

b **CD3** ▶ **10** **PRONUNCIATION** Listen and practise.

Melanie

HELP WITH GRAMMAR
Past Simple of *be*: positive and negative

3 **a** Look at these sentences. Are they in the present or the past?

I **was** at the World Cup Final.

We **were** near the Opera House.

The stadium **wasn't** full.

They **weren't** very happy.

b Look at the sentences in **3a** again. Then fill in the gaps in the table with *was*, *wasn't*, *were* and *weren't*.

POSITIVE (+)	NEGATIVE (−)
I _____	I **wasn't** (= was not)
you **were**	you **weren't** (= were not)
he / she / it **was**	he / she / it _____
we _____	we **weren't**
they **were**	they _____

TIP • The past of *there is / there are* is *there was / there were*.

`GRAMMAR 8.1` ▸ p129

4 `CD3` ▸ 12 `PRONUNCIATION` Listen and practise. Notice how we say *was* and *were*.

I was /wəz/ at the World Cup Final.
We were /wə/ near the Opera House.

5 **a** Choose the correct words.

1 I *was / were* only thirteen at the time.
2 My sisters *wasn't / weren't* at the concert.
3 There *was / were* a lot of people in Sydney that night.
4 John Lennon *was / were* a great musician.
5 The fireworks *was / were* on TV in lots of countries.
6 It *was / were* my first World Cup.
7 There *wasn't / weren't* any empty seats in the stadium.
8 At 3 a.m. my parents *was / were* very tired, but I *wasn't / weren't*.
9 The concert *wasn't / weren't* very expensive – my ticket *was / were* only $4.50!

b Work in pairs. Compare answers. Who says each sentence: Melanie, Tania or Diego?

Get ready ... Get it right!

6 Work in groups of three. Look at p96.

I was in Sydney on New Year's Eve 1999. I was only twelve, and I was there with my mum and dad. We were near the Opera House all evening, and at midnight there were some amazing fireworks. Then there was a big party in the city all night. It was a fantastic New Year!

Tanya

I was at the World Cup Final in Johannesburg in 2010. I was very young at the time. There were 85,000 people in the stadium and I was there with a friend from Holland and his dad. They weren't very happy at the end because it was Spain 1 Holland 0, but I was! It was a great match – and I was there!

Diego

Vocabulary years and past time phrases
Grammar Past Simple of *be*: questions and short answers; *was born* / *were born*

Years and past time phrases

1 a Work in pairs. Match 1–6 to a–f.

1	1887	a	nineteen eighty
2	1900	b	twenty ten
3	1980	c	eighteen eighty-seven
4	2000	d	two thousand and nine
5	2009	e	nineteen hundred
6	2010	f	two thousand

TIP • We use *in* with years: *in 1980*, etc.

b CD3▷13 **PRONUNCIATION** Listen and practise.

c Work with your partner. Say these years.

2013	1977	2018	1815	1990	2003

2 a Match pictures A–D to sentences 1–4.

1 Joe was in Paris **last** week.
2 He's at work **now**.
3 He was in bed four hours **ago**.
4 He was at home **yesterday** afternoon.

b CD3▷14 **PRONUNCIATION** Listen and practise sentences 1–4.

3 Fill in the gaps with *yesterday*, *in*, *last* or *ago*.

1 I was in a café two hours _ago_ .
2 I was at home _____ night.
3 I wasn't in this country _____ 1999.
4 I wasn't at work _____ morning.
5 I was in this class _____ month.
6 I wasn't in this class three months _____ .

An Indian wedding

4 a Check these words with your teacher.

a wedding	a bride	a groom	a wedding anniversary

b Look at the photo of an Indian wedding. Which person is the bride? Which person is the groom?

c CD3▷15 Listen to Sunil talk to a friend about his wedding. Choose the correct words in these sentences.

1 Sunil and Pria's wedding anniversary is on *Saturday* / *Sunday*.
2 Their wedding was *five* / *ten* years ago.
3 Their wedding was in *the UK* / *India*.
4 Sunil's parents *were* / *weren't* at the wedding.
5 There *was* / *wasn't* a party after the wedding.

d Listen again. Answer these questions.

1 Where was the wedding?
2 How old were Sunil and Pria on their wedding day?
3 How many people were at the wedding?
4 Where was Sunil's sister?
5 Were Sunil's brothers at the wedding?
6 How many days was the party?

HELP WITH GRAMMAR Past Simple of *be*: questions and short answers; *was born* / *were born*

5 **a** Look at these questions. Notice the word order.

WH- QUESTIONS (?)

Where	was	the wedding?
How old	were	Sunil and Pria?

b Write these questions in the table.

1 How many people **were** at the wedding?

2 Where **was** Sunil's sister?

c Fill in the gaps with *was*, *were*, *wasn't* or *weren't*.

YES / NO QUESTIONS (?)	SHORT ANSWERS
Was I / he / she / it at the wedding?	Yes, I / he / she / it _____ .
	No, I / he / she / it _____ .
_____ you / we / they at the wedding?	Yes, you / we / they _____ .
	No, you / we / they _____ .

WAS BORN / *WERE BORN*

d Fill in the gaps with *was* or *were*.

1 **A** Where _____ Pria born?
  B She _____ born in London.

2 **A** When _____ you born?
  B I _____ born in 1991.

GRAMMAR 8.2 ▶ p129

6 CD3 ▶ 16 PRONUNCIATION Listen and practise the questions and answers in **5**.

Where was the wedding?
How old were Sunil and Pria?

7 **a** Choose the correct words.

1 Who *was* / *were* the bride and groom?

2 *Was* / *Were* they the same age?

3 When *was* / *were* the wedding?

4 *Was* / *Were* Sunil's parents at the wedding?

5 Who *was* / *were* in the USA?

6 Where *was* / *were* Pria born?

b Work in pairs. Ask and answer the questions.

8 **a** Make questions with these words.

1 you / last / at home / Sunday / Were ?

2 evening / you / yesterday / were / Where ?

3 three / you / months / on / Were / ago / holiday ?

4 New Year's Eve 1999 / you / on / were / Where ?

5 at work / last / Were / Monday / you ?

6 you / were / Where / born ?

b Work in pairs. Ask and answer the questions.

9 **a** Write the names of three people you know. Think when and where they were born. Don't write this information.

b Work in pairs. Ask about the people on your partner's paper.

Who's Karima?	She's my sister.

When was she born?	In 1997.

Where was she born?	In Dubai.

Get ready ... Get it right!

10 Work in new pairs. Student A p88. Student B p93.

> **QUICK REVIEW Past Simple of *be*** Work in pairs. Ask your partner where he or she was: three hours ago, yesterday afternoon, last Saturday, at 11 a.m., last Sunday, last New Year's Eve. **A** *Where were you three hours ago?* **B** *I was at work.*

Months and dates

1 a CD3 ▶ 17 **PRONUNCIATION** Listen and practise the months.

January   February   March
April   May   June   July
August   September   October
November   December

b Work in pairs. Say a month. Your partner says the next two months.

> March

> April, May

2 a CD3 ▶ 18 **PRONUNCIATION** Listen and practise these dates. Notice the letters in **pink**.

1**st**	fir**st**	6**th**	six**th**	11**th**	eleven**th**
2**nd**	seco**nd**	7**th**	seven**th**	12**th**	twelf**th**
3**rd**	thi**rd**	8**th**	eigh**th**	20**th**	twentie**th**
4**th**	four**th**	9**th**	nin**th**	21**st**	twenty-fir**st**
5**th**	fif**th**	10**th**	ten**th**	30**th**	thirtie**th**

b Work in pairs. Say these dates.

13**th**	14**th**	15**th**	16**th**	17**th**	18**th**
19**th**	22**nd**	23**rd**	24**th**	25**th**	26**th**
27**th**	28**th**	29**th**	31**st**		

c CD3 ▶ 19 **PRONUNCIATION** Listen and check. Listen again and practise.

REAL WORLD Talking about days and dates

3 Read these questions and answers. Notice the words in bold.

1 **A** What day is it today?
  B (It's) Monday.
2 **A** What's the date today?
  B (It's) March **the** seventh.
3 **A** When's your birthday?
  B (It's **on**) June **the** second.

REAL WORLD 8.1 ▶ p129

4 CD3 ▶ 20 **PRONUNCIATION** Listen and practise the questions and answers in **3**.

5 CD3 ▶ 21 Listen to four conversations. Which dates do you hear?

1 June *20th* / *22nd*   3 October *3rd* / *23rd*
2 March *13th* / *30th*   4 April *1st* / *4th*

6 a Write five dates (*March 3rd*, *August 25th*, etc.).

b Work in pairs. Say the dates. Write your partner's dates. Are they correct?

c Ask other students when their birthdays are. Do any students have birthdays in the same month as you?

> When's your birthday, Adela?

> It's on May 25th.

> My birthday's on May 22nd.

Happy birthday!

7 a Check these words with your teacher.

> a present   a driving test
> go to a club   meet   decide

b **VIDEO** ▶ 8 CD3 ▶ 22 Look at the photo of Danny and Karen. Listen to their conversation. What do they decide to do this evening?

c Work in pairs. How much can you remember? Choose the correct words or phrases.

1 Karen orders *an egg sandwich /* (*a croissant*).
2 *Danny / Karen* has a driving test at *10.30 / 11.30*.
3 Danny's birthday was *yesterday / last week*.
4 There's a *Mexican / Italian* restaurant near *Karen's / Danny's* flat.
5 *Karen / Danny* goes to the restaurant *every week / every month*.
6 They decide to meet at the *café / cinema* at *seven o'clock / half past seven*.

d Watch or listen again. Check your answers.

REAL WORLD
Making suggestions

8 Read this conversation. Fill in the gaps with these words.

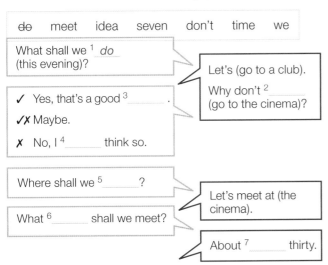

~~do~~   meet   idea   seven   don't   time   we

What shall we ¹ *do* (this evening)?

Let's (go to a club).
Why don't ² _____ (go to the cinema)?

✓ Yes, that's a good ³ _____ .
✓✗ Maybe.
✗ No, I ⁴ _____ think so.

Where shall we ⁵ _____ ?

Let's meet at (the cinema).

What ⁶ _____ shall we meet?

About ⁷ _____ thirty.

REAL WORLD 8.2 ▶ p129

9 CD3 ▶ 23 PRONUNCIATION Listen and practise the sentences in **8**.

What shall we do this evening?
Let's go to a club.

10 a Put this conversation in order.

GEORGE

a What shall we do tomorrow evening, Jessica?   *1*
b Great! See you there!
c No, I don't think so.
d OK. What time shall we meet?
e Yes, that's a good idea. Where shall we meet?

JESSICA

f Let's meet at the restaurant.
g Why don't we go to the cinema?   *2*
h About quarter to eight.
i OK. Let's go to that Indian restaurant in Old Street.

b CD3 ▶ 24 Listen and check.

c Work in pairs. Practise the conversation in **10a**.

11 a Work in new pairs. Write a conversation about next Saturday. Use phrases in **8** and your own ideas.

b Practise your conversation until you can remember it.

c Work in groups of four. Take turns to role-play your conversations. What do the other pair decide to do on Saturday?

d Role-play one of your group's conversations for the class.

Danny   *Karen*

VOCABULARY
8D AND SKILLS

Life's a party!

Vocabulary big numbers
Skills Reading and Listening:
fantastic festivals; Listening:
two festivals

QUICK REVIEW **Making suggestions** Work in pairs. You want to go out together tomorrow evening. Make suggestions about what to do. Decide a place and time to meet. **A** *What shall we do tomorrow evening?* **B** *Why don't we ... ?*

1 a Match the numbers in A to the phrases in B.

A	B
150	a thousand
390	a million
1,000	sixteen thousand, two hundred
16,200	a hundred and fifty
750,000	fifty million
1,000,000	three hundred and ninety
50,000,000	seven hundred and fifty thousand

b **CD3 25** **PRONUNCIATION** Listen and practise.

2 a **CD3 26** Listen and write the numbers.

b Work in pairs. Compare answers.

3 a Work on your own. Write five big numbers.

b Work in new pairs. Say your numbers. Write your partner's numbers. Are they correct?

4 a Check these words with your teacher.

| a festival | throw | a kilo | garlic | samba |

b Read the article. Fill in the gaps with these numbers.

| 70 million | 5 million | 177,500 | 125,000 |
| 150,000 | 30,000 | 1,500 | |

c **CD3 27** Listen to the article and check your answers.

5 Read the article again. Answer these questions.

1 When and where is La Tomatina?

2 What do people do there?

3 What do people do at the festival in Ivrea?

4 When is the Gilroy Garlic Festival?

5 What food do people eat at this festival?

6 When was the first Glastonbury Festival?

7 What do people do at Carnival in Brazil?

8 How many days was the 2013 Kumbh Mela?

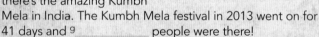

Fantastic festivals

There are lots of fantastic festivals around the world that you can visit. For example, on the last Wednesday in August every year, a _____ people travel to Buñol, in Spain, for La Tomatina. At this festival people throw tomatoes at each other – b _____ kilos of them!

There's also a similar festival in Italy, where the people of the town of Ivrea throw oranges at each other for three days. And every July c _____ people go to Gilroy, in California, for the Gilroy Garlic Festival. Here you can eat garlic bread, garlic chicken, garlic chocolate – and garlic ice cream!

Of course, not all festivals are about food. The UK's favourite music festival is the Glastonbury Festival. Only d _____ people were at the first Glastonbury Festival in June 1970, but in 2011 there were e _____ people there. And of course there's Carnival in Brazil, which is in February or March every year. In cities all over the country, people dance in the street to samba bands all day and all night. Every year about f _____ people enjoy Carnival in the streets of Rio de Janeiro. And if you want to go to a really big festival, there's the amazing Kumbh Mela in India. The Kumbh Mela festival in 2013 went on for 41 days and g _____ people were there!

Glastonbury

Rio Carnival

6 Work in pairs. Which festivals in the article would you like to go to? Which wouldn't you like to go to?

7 a **CD3** 28 Close your books. Listen to Ella and Owen. Which festivals in the article do they talk about?

b Listen again. Choose the correct answers.

1 Ella goes to about *three / four* festivals every year.
2 She likes Glastonbury because there are lots of different *bands / things you can do*.
3 She thinks the best thing about the festival is *the music / the people you meet*.
4 Owen went to Brazil in *February / March*.
5 He *loves / doesn't like* Brazilian music.
6 It was *easy / difficult* to sleep in the hotel.
7 He *can / can't* samba very well.
8 He has lots of *photos / new friends* from the festival.

HELP WITH LISTENING Linking (2)

8 a **CD3** 29 Listen to these sentences from Ella and Owen's conversation. Why do we link the words in **pink** and **blue**?

There_are lots_of different things you can do.
I love sitting_in cafés_and talking to people.
There were thousands_of people_in the street.
But_I have_a lot_of new friends from the festival.

b Look at Audio Script **CD3** 28 p112. Listen to the whole conversation again and notice the consonant–vowel linking.

9 a Work in groups. Which festivals are there in your town, city or country? What do people do there?

b Tell the class about one festival in your town, city or country.

Kumbh Mela

HELP WITH PRONUNCIATION /ɔ:/ and /ɜ:/

1 **CD3** 30 Look at the pictures. Listen to the sounds and words. Listen again and practise.

 /ɔ:/
 /ɜ:/

forty   burger

2 **CD3** 31 Listen to these words. Notice how we say the **pink** and **blue** letters. Listen again and practise.

/ɔ:/	/ɜ:/
forty four sport	burger first work
boring awful August	shirt skirt Turkish
daughter small always	German girl early
morning water short	thirty third surname

3 a **CD3** 32 Listen and practise these sentences.

1 It's the thirty-first of August.
2 It was a boring morning at work.
3 This small burger is awful.
4 The Turkish girl is always early.
5 It's a German sports company.
6 My daughter has forty-four skirts and thirty-three shirts!

b Work in pairs. Practise the sentences.

continue2learn

▶ **Vocabulary, Grammar and Real World**

■ Extra Practice 8 and Progress Portfolio 8 p104
■ **Language Summary 8** p128
■ **8A–D** Workbook p38
■ **Self-study DVD-ROM 8** with Review Video

▶ **Reading and Writing**

■ **Portfolio 8** Going out Workbook p66
Reading entertainment adverts; emails
Writing *a/an* and *the*; your last film, play or rock concert

Transport

1 **a** Tick (✓) the words you know. Then
check new words in **VOCABULARY 9.1** ▶ p130.

> a car   a bus   a train   a taxi   a bike
> a motorbike   a plane   a boat

b **CD3**▶**33** **PRONUNCIATION** Listen and
practise.

c Underline the verbs in these
sentences.

1 I usually go to work by car.
2 I come to this school by bus.
3 I never travel by plane.
4 I always walk to work.

TIP • We travel *by car*, *by bus*, etc.

2 **a** Write sentences about you.

1 I … to work / school / university …
   I always go to work by bus.
2 I usually … to this school …
3 When I go shopping, I usually …
4 I love travelling …
5 I don't like travelling …
6 I never travel …

b Work in pairs. Say your sentences.
Are any the same?

Bangkok to Brighton

3 **a** Check these words with your teacher.

> a tuk-tuk   a journey
> raise money for charity

b Look at the photos and map. What is
the article about, do you think?

c Read the article. Are your guesses
correct?

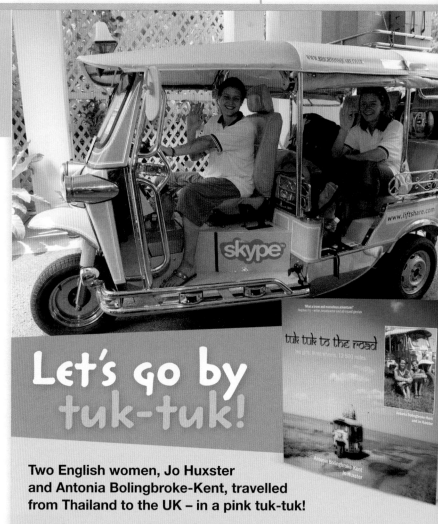

Let's go by tuk-tuk!

**Two English women, Jo Huxster
and Antonia Bolingbroke-Kent, travelled
from Thailand to the UK – in a pink tuk-tuk!**

Jo **had** the idea when she **went** to Bangkok on holiday. When she **came**
back to England, she **told** her friend Antonia what she **wanted** to do.
Antonia **liked** the idea, so they went back to Bangkok and **bought** a
tuk-tuk called Ting Tong. Jo and Antonia **started** their journey on May 28th
2006. They travelled for 12 hours every day, usually on very bad roads.
All the people they **met** were very friendly and they sometimes **gave** Jo
and Antonia food and money. The two women travelled 12,500 miles and
visited 12 countries. They **arrived** in Brighton, in the UK, 98 days after they
left Bangkok. After they **got** home, they **wrote** a book called *Tuk-Tuk to the
Road*. They also raised £50,000 for charity.

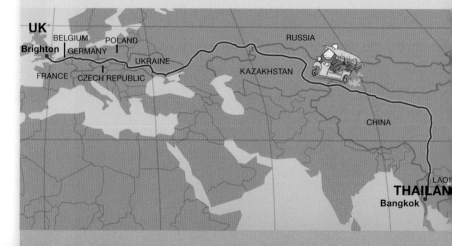

4 Read the article again. Complete the table with the correct dates, places and numbers.

a	travelled by	*tuk-tuk*
b	date started	
c	place started	
d	place finished	
e	miles travelled	
f	countries visited	*12*
g	days travelled	
h	money raised	

HELP WITH GRAMMAR Past Simple: positive (regular and irregular verbs)

5 a Look at the regular Past Simple forms in **blue** in the article. Then complete these rules with *-d* or *-ed*.

REGULAR VERBS

● To make the Past Simple of regular verbs, we usually add _____ to the verb.

● For regular verbs that end in *-e* (*like*, *arrive*, etc.), we add _____ to the verb.

TIP ● The Past Simple of *travel* is *travelled*.

b Look at the irregular Past Simple forms in **pink** in the article. Match them to verbs 1–10.

IRREGULAR VERBS

1 buy	*bought*	6 have	_____
2 come	_____	7 leave	_____
3 get	_____	8 meet	_____
4 give	_____	9 tell	_____
5 go	_____	10 write	_____

TIP ● The Past Simple of regular and irregular verbs is the same for *I, you, he, she, it, we* and *they*.

c Check in GRAMMAR 9.1 ▸ p131. Learn the other irregular verbs in the table.

6 a Write the Past Simple forms of these regular verbs.

1 visit	*visited*	7 live	_____
2 watch	_____	8 want	_____
3 play	_____	9 love	_____
4 hate	_____	10 talk	_____
5 walk	_____	11 start	_____
6 work	_____	12 finish	_____

b CD3 ▸ 34 PRONUNCIATION Listen and practise. Which Past Simple forms end in /ɪd/?

c CD3 ▸ 35 PRONUNCIATION Listen and practise the irregular Past Simple forms in **5b**.

HELP WITH LISTENING
Present Simple or Past Simple

7 a CD3 ▸ 36 Listen to these sentences. Notice the difference between the **Present Simple** and the **Past Simple**.

1 I **live** in London. I **lived** in London.
2 We **work** at home. We **worked** at home.
3 They **love** it. They **loved** it.

b CD3 ▸ 37 Listen to six pairs of sentences. Which do you hear first, the Present Simple or the Past Simple?

1 Past Simple

Around the world by bike

8 a Read about Mark Beaumont's journey. Fill in the gaps with the Past Simple of the verbs in brackets.

b Work in pairs. Compare answers.

Mark Beaumont, from Scotland, ¹ *cycled* (cycle) around the world in only 194 days and 17 hours. Mark ² _____ (have) the idea after he ³ _____ (leave) Glasgow University in 2007, and he ⁴ _____ (start) his journey in Paris on August 5ᵗʰ the same year.

He ⁵ _____ (travel) 18,300 miles and ⁶ _____ (visit) twenty countries, and he ⁷ _____ (meet) a lot of interesting people. He also ⁸ _____ (write) an online diary and ⁹ _____ (get) emails from friends and family every week. Mark ¹⁰ _____ (finish) his journey in Paris on February 15ᵗʰ 2008. His family ¹¹ _____ (go) to Paris for the big day, and his mother ¹² _____ (tell) the newspapers she ¹³ _____ (be) very proud of her son. Mark also ¹⁴ _____ (raise) over £10,000 for charity.

Get ready ... Get it right!

9 Work in groups of three. Look at p96.

9B ▶ My last holiday

Vocabulary holiday activities
Grammar Past Simple: negative,
questions and short answers

QUICK REVIEW Past Simple Write five regular or irregular verbs and their Past Simple forms. Work in pairs. Take turns to say the verbs. Your partner says a sentence with the Past Simple form: **A** *go* **B** *I went out with friends last night*.

Holiday activities

1 **a** Work in pairs. Tick (✓) the phrases you know. Then do the exercise in VOCABULARY 9.2 ▶ p130.

> go on holiday   take photos   go to the beach
> stay with friends or family   stay in a hotel
> go sightseeing   go swimming   go for a walk
> rent a car   travel around   have a good time

b CD3 ▶ 38 PRONUNCIATION Listen and practise.

c Work with your partner. What are the Past Simple forms of the verbs in **1a**?

go → went   take → took

2 **a** Write four sentences about things you do on holiday. Use *always*, *usually*, *sometimes* and phrases from **1a**.

I always go to the beach.
I usually stay with friends.

b Work in pairs. Say your sentences. Are any of your partner's sentences true for you?

Favourite places

3 **a** Check these words with your teacher.

> a palace   the sea   the scenery

b CD3 ▶ 39 Read and listen to Heidi, Charlie and John. Match the people to the photos on p73. Which countries are the places in?

c Read about the holidays again. Fill in the gaps in these sentences with *Heidi*, *Charlie*, *John* or *Diane*.

1 *Charlie* visited a beautiful old palace.
2 _____ stayed with some friends.
3 _____ stayed by the sea.
4 _____ only went to one city.
5 _____ and _____ went for a walk every day.
6 _____ and _____ went on holiday last year.
7 _____ , _____ and _____ stayed in hotels.

Heidi

I went on holiday to Moscow last year. I didn't stay in a hotel, I stayed with some friends. I went sightseeing in the mornings and I took a lot of photos. My favourite place was Red Square. There are a lot of beautiful buildings and it's a great place to watch people. I was only in Russia for a week, so I didn't visit any other places. Next time, maybe!

Charlie

Last year I travelled around Spain on holiday. My favourite place was Granada, a very friendly city in the south. When I was there I visited the Alhambra, a beautiful old palace – that was fantastic! I also went to Valencia, a very interesting city by the sea. I stayed in a nice hotel and went to the beach every afternoon. But I didn't go swimming because I can't swim!

John and Diane

We didn't go on holiday last year, but two years ago we went to Turkey. We rented a car and travelled around the country for two weeks. Our favourite place was Cappadocia – the scenery there is amazing. We stayed in a small hotel and went for a walk every morning. We didn't stay there for very long, but we took about 500 photos!

HELP WITH GRAMMAR Past Simple: negative

4 **a** Look at these sentences. Notice the word order.

I	didn't	stay	in a hotel.	(didn't
He	didn't	go	swimming.	= did not)

b Write these sentences in the table.

1 She **didn't visit** any other places.
2 We **didn't go** on holiday last year.
3 They **didn't stay** there for very long.

GRAMMAR 9.2 ▶ p131

Cappadocia

Red Square

the Alhambra

5 **CD3** ▶ 40 **PRONUNCIATION** Listen and practise the sentences in **4**.

I didn't stay in a hotel.

6 **a** Make these sentences negative. Write the correct sentences.

1 **a** Heidi went to Prague.
   Heidi didn't go to Prague. She went to Moscow.
   b She went sightseeing in the afternoons.

2 **a** Charlie went to Spain two years ago.
   b He stayed with friends in Valencia.

3 **a** John and Diane rented bikes for two weeks.
   b They stayed in a big hotel in Cappadocia.

b Work in pairs. Compare sentences.

7 Cover the texts. Then answer these questions.

1 Where did Heidi go on holiday?
2 Who did she stay with?
3 When did Charlie go to the beach?
4 Did he go swimming?
5 Did John and Diane visit Turkey last year?
6 How many photos did they take?

HELP WITH GRAMMAR Past Simple: questions and short answers

8 **a** Look at these questions. Notice the word order.

WH- QUESTIONS (?)

Where	did	Heidi	go	on holiday?
Who	did	she	stay	with?

b Write these questions in the table.

1 When **did** Charlie **go** to the beach?
2 How many photos **did** they **take**?

c Fill in the gaps with *did* or *didn't*.

YES / NO QUESTIONS (?)	SHORT ANSWERS
Did he go swimming?	Yes, he _____ . No, he _____ .
_____ they visit Turkey last year?	Yes, they _____ . No, they _____ .

GRAMMAR 9.3 ▶ **p131**

9 **CD3** ▶ 41 **PRONUNCIATION** Listen and practise the questions and short answers in **8**.

10 Work in pairs. Student A p90. Student B p95.

Get ready … Get it right!

11 **a** Make Past Simple questions with *you*.

● When … last go on holiday?
   When did you last go on holiday?
● Where … go?
● What … do there?
● Who … go with?
● Where … stay?
● How … travel around?
● … have a good time?

b Answer the questions for you.

12 **a** Work in pairs. Ask your partner the questions.

b Tell the class about your partner's holiday.

▶ REAL WORLD
9C
A weekend away

Vocabulary at the station
Real World buying train tickets;
asking about last weekend

QUICK REVIEW Holiday activities Write four things people do on holiday (*stay in a hotel*, etc.). Work in pairs. Compare lists. Then talk about your favourite holiday.

Sally

At the station

1 **a** Work in pairs. Look at the photos. Match these words to 1–6.

> a customer 1   a single ☐   a return ☐
> a ticket office ☐   a ticket machine ☐   a platform ☐

b CD3 ▶42 PRONUNCIATION Listen and practise.

2 VIDEO ▶9.1 CD3 ▶43 It's Saturday morning. Sally is at the station. Watch or listen to her conversation with the ticket seller. Where does Sally want to go? How much is her ticket?

REAL WORLD Buying train tickets

3 VIDEO ▶9.1 CD3 ▶43 Watch or listen again. Fill in the gaps.

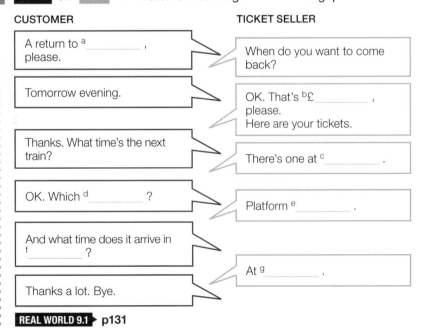

CUSTOMER

A return to ªˍˍˍˍˍˍ, please.

Tomorrow evening.

Thanks. What time's the next train?

OK. Which ᵈˍˍˍˍˍˍ?

And what time does it arrive in ᶠˍˍˍˍˍˍ?

Thanks a lot. Bye.

TICKET SELLER

When do you want to come back?

OK. That's ᵇ£ˍˍˍˍˍˍ, please.
Here are your tickets.

There's one at ᶜˍˍˍˍˍˍ.

Platform ᵉˍˍˍˍˍˍ.

At ᵍˍˍˍˍˍ.

REAL WORLD 9.1 ▶ p131

4 CD3 ▶44 PRONUNCIATION Listen and practise the sentences in **3**.

5 **a** Work in pairs. Practise the conversation in **3**. Take turns to be the customer.

b Close your books. Practise the conversation again.

6 **a** Read this conversation. Choose the correct words.

CUSTOMER A single ¹(*to*) / *from* Oxford, please.

TICKET SELLER OK. ²*That* / *That's* £18.60, please. Here's ³*you* / *your* ticket.

C Thanks. What time's the ⁴*next* / *near* train?

TS There's one ⁵*at* / *on* 11.52.

C ⁶*Which* / *Where* platform?

TS Platform 1.

C What time ⁷*do* / *does* it arrive in Oxford?

TS ⁸*In* / *At* 12.47.

C Thanks ⁹*much* / *a lot*. Bye.

b CD3 ▶45 Listen and check.

c Work in pairs. Practise the conversation. Take turns to be the customer.

7 Work in new pairs. Student A p90. Student B p95.

Last weekend

8 a **VIDEO** ▶9.2 **CD3** ▶46 It's Monday morning. Watch or listen to Rob and Sally talk about last weekend. Put photos A–D in the order they talk about them.

b Work in pairs. How much can you remember? Choose the correct words or phrases.

1 Sally went to see her (brother) / sister last weekend.
2 They went shopping on *Saturday* / *Sunday* afternoon.
3 They *enjoyed* / *didn't enjoy* their evening at the theatre.
4 *Sally* / *Her brother* doesn't like art galleries very much.
5 They had lunch with *some friends* / *their parents*.
6 Rob went to a *Turkish* / *Spanish* restaurant on Saturday.

c Watch or listen again. Check your answers.

REAL WORLD Asking about last weekend

9 Fill in the gaps in questions 1–7 with these words.

| ~~have~~ | you | did | What | do | good | Where |

1 Did you *have* a good weekend?
2 _____ did you do at the weekend?
3 _____ did you go?
4 What did you _____ there?
5 Did you have a _____ time?
6 What _____ you see?
7 Did _____ enjoy it?

REAL WORLD 9.2 ▶ **p131**

10 **CD3** ▶47 **PRONUNCIATION** Listen and practise the questions in **9**.

Did you háve a gŏod weekĕnd?

11 a Make notes about things you did last weekend.

went for a walk   played tennis   watched TV

b Work in pairs. Ask your partner about last weekend. Use questions from **9** and your own questions. Give more information if possible.

What did you do last weekend?

I went for a walk.

Where did you go?

c Tell the class about one thing your partner did last weekend.

Rob   Sally

Leicester Square

Oxford Street

The West End

The National Gallery

9D VOCABULARY AND SKILLS

Who, what, when?

Vocabulary question words
Skills Reading: a quiz;
Listening: How many did I get right?

QUICK REVIEW Past Simple *yes/no* questions **Work in pairs. Ask questions about yesterday.**
Find five things you both did: A *Did you eat out yesterday?* **B** *Yes, I did.* **A** *Me too.*

1 **a** Check these words with your teacher.

> a billion   the Earth   the moon   a director   the President   earn

b Work in pairs. Do the quiz.

2 **CD3** ▶ 48 Listen to Jackie and Mark do the quiz. Tick the correct answers in the quiz. How many answers did you get right?

HOW MUCH DO YOU KNOW ?

5 **When did the first man walk on the moon?**
a 1949
b 1969
c 1989

1 **What is the capital of Australia?**
a Canberra
b Sydney
c Melbourne

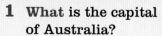

6 **How much does the President of the USA earn a year?**
a $400,000
b $700,000
c $1 million

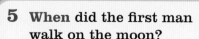

2 **Where were the 2008 Olympic Games?**
a London
b Athens
c Beijing

7 **How many countries are there in Africa?**
a Fourteen
b Thirty-four
c Fifty-four

3 **How old is the Earth?**
a 10 billion years old
b 4½ billion years old
c 1½ billion years old

8 **Why is the English town of Stratford-upon-Avon famous?**
a Because Harry Potter went to school there
b Because the world's first football match was played there
c Because the writer William Shakespeare was born there

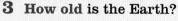

4 **Who was the director of the films *Jaws*, *E.T.* and *Jurassic Park*?**
a James Cameron
b Martin Scorsese
c Steven Spielberg

HELP WITH LISTENING Sentence stress (3)

3 **a** `CD3` ▶48 Read and listen to the beginning of the conversation. Notice the sentence stress. We stress the important words.

JACKIE Mark, do you want to do a quiz?

MARK Yes, I love doing quizzes. What's the first question?

JACKIE OK. What is the capital of Australia? Is it Canberra, Sydney or Melbourne?

b Look at Audio Script `CD3` ▶48 p113. Listen to the whole conversation and follow the sentence stress. How many questions did Mark get right?

HELP WITH VOCABULARY Question words

4 Look at the question words in **pink** in the quiz. Match the words to the things they ask about.

Who —————— a thing
What ————— a person
When   a reason (*because* …)
Where   an amount of money (*£50*, etc.)
Why   a place
How old   a time
How many   age
How much   a number

VOCABULARY 9.4 ▶ p130

5 **a** Choose the correct words.

1 (*When*) / *Who* did you last go to the cinema?
2 *What* / *Where* did you do last Friday?
3 *How old* / *How many* is your mobile phone?
4 *How many* / *How much* people live in your house or flat?
5 *When* / *Who* was your first English teacher?
6 *Why* / *What* do you want to learn English?
7 *Who* / *Where* were your parents born?
8 *When* / *Who* did you last go to a concert?
9 *How many* / *How much* brothers and sisters do you have?
10 *How many* / *How much* do you spend on travel?

b Work in pairs. Take turns to ask the questions in **5a**. Ask more questions if possible.

> When did you last go to the cinema?

> About three weeks ago.

> What did you see?

6 **a** Write four questions with *you* to ask another student. Use the question words in **4**.

b Work in new pairs. Take turns to ask your questions. Ask more questions if possible.

c Tell the class two things about your partner.

HELP WITH PRONUNCIATION /l/ and /r/

1 `CD3` ▶49 Look at the pictures. Listen to the sounds and words. Listen again and practise.

leave   arrive

2 `CD3` ▶50 Listen to these words. Notice how we say the **pink** and **blue** consonants. Listen again and practise.

/l/	/r/
leave plane flying	arrive train read
like England place	write price Russia
dollars holiday wallet	around very married
travelling classroom	travelling classroom

3 **a** Sometimes we don't say the letter *r* in British English. Look at these words. Which *r*s do we say (✓)? Which don't we say (✗)?

friend ✓	first ✗	doctor	green	morning
radio	sport	park	right	theatre
fruit	start	tomorrow	great	terrible

b `CD3` ▶51 Listen and check. Listen again and practise.

continue2learn

▶ Vocabulary, Grammar and Real World
- **Extra Practice 9** and **Progress Portfolio 9** p105
- **Language Summary 9** p130
- **9A–D** Workbook p43
- **Self-study DVD-ROM 9** with Review Video

▶ Reading and Writing
- **Portfolio 9** On holiday Workbook p68
  Reading a travel blog; a holiday in France
  Writing *because*, *so*, *when*; your last holiday

Future plans

1 **a** Work in pairs. Fill in the gaps with these verbs. Then check in VOCABULARY 10.1 > p132.

> ~~start~~   look for   get   do   leave   move

start < school or university / a new job

_____ < school or university / your job

_____ < a (computer) course / an exam

_____ < house / to another city or country

_____ < engaged / married

_____ < a house or a flat / a (new) job

b CD3 52 PRONUNCIATION Listen and practise the phrases in **1a**.

c Work in new pairs. Test your partner.

> a course   do a course

A world language

2 **a** CD3 53 Look at the photos. Read and listen to Isabella, Kamil, Ali and Colette. Where does each person study English?

b Read the texts again. Fill in the gaps with *Isabella*, *Kamil*, *Ali* and *Colette*.

1   _Isabella_ is going to get married next year.
2   _____ is going to do a computer course.
3   _____ is going to travel around the UK.
4   _____ is going to move to Sydney.
5   _____ is going to look for a job.
6   _____ is going to start a new job.
7   _____ is going to move to Rio.

Isabella from Brazil

I study English at the University of São Paulo. My boyfriend, Gustavo, is also a student here. He studies medicine and he's going to be a doctor. We're going to get married next year. But we aren't going to live in São Paulo, we're going to move to Rio, where my family lives.

Kamil from Poland

I do English at school. It's my favourite subject and I want to study it at university. I'm going to leave school in June, but I'm not going to start university this year. First I'm going to do a computer course here in Kraków and then I'm going to look for a job in the UK.

Ali from Egypt

I'm at an English language school in Cambridge. We have classes for five hours every day! Next month my sister is going to visit me and we're going to travel around the UK. She isn't going to stay here for very long, only two weeks. Then I'm going to start a new job in Cairo.

HELP WITH GRAMMAR
be going to: positive and negative

3 **a** Look again at the sentences in **2b**. Then choose the correct phrase in this rule.

- We use ***be going to* + verb** to talk about *the past / the present / future plans*.

b Look at these sentences. Notice the word order.

POSITIVE (+)

I	'm	going to	do	a computer course.

NEGATIVE (–)

I	'm not	going to	start	university this year.

c Write these sentences in the correct tables.
1 He's **going to leave** his job.
2 She isn't **going to stay** here for very long.
3 We're **going to travel** around the UK.
4 They aren't **going to live** in São Paulo.

GRAMMAR 10.1 ► p133

4 **CD3** ►54 **PRONUNCIATION** Listen and practise the sentences in **3**.

do a computer course →
I'm going to /tə/ *do a computer course.*

5 **a** Look again at the texts about Isabella, Kamil, Ali and Colette. Underline all the sentences with *be going to*.

b Work in pairs. Compare answers. Which sentences are negative?

Colette from France

My husband, Oliver, is Australian, so we sometimes speak English together at home. I also study English online for four hours a week and I'm going to do an exam next month. Our two daughters live with us now, but they're going to move to Paris in September. And next year Oliver's going to leave his job and we're going to move to Sydney!

6 **a** Fill in the gaps with the correct form of *be going to* and the verbs in brackets.

1
a We *'re going to visit* London and Bath. (visit)
b She _____ in the UK for two weeks. (stay)
2
a They _____ a flat together. (look for)
b We _____ a house near the beach. (buy)
3
a He _____ university next year. (leave)
b We _____ a big wedding. (not have)
4
a I _____ my exams in June. (do)
b I _____ a job in London. (not look for)

b Work in pairs. Compare answers. Then match the sentences to the people in the photos.

Future time phrases

7 **a** Put these future time phrases in order.

> tonight [1]   in June next year [ ]   next month [ ]
> in 2025 [ ]   tomorrow morning [ ]   next week [ ]

b Write three sentences about things that your family and friends are going to do in the future. Use words and phrases from **7a** and your own ideas.

My friend Jin is going to start a new job next week.

c Work in pairs. Take turns to tell your partner your sentences.

Get ready … Get it right!

8 Write one thing you're going to do: after class, tomorrow evening, next Sunday, next week, next month, next year.

meet some friends after class
watch a football match tomorrow evening

9 **a** Work in groups. Talk about your plans. Are any the same?

> I'm going to meet some friends after class.
>
> Me too.

b Tell the class about your group's plans.

> Meltem and I are going to meet some friends after class.

QUICK REVIEW Future plans Write one phrase for these verbs: *start, leave, do, move, get, look for* (*start a new job*, etc.). Work in pairs. Compare phrases. Then say when you are going to do some of the things on your lists: *I'm going to start a new job next month*.

Phrases with *have, watch, go, go to*

1 a Work in pairs. Match these words or phrases to the correct verbs. Then check in VOCABULARY 10.3 ▶ p132.

> dinner with friends   the cinema
> shopping   TV   swimming   the news
> coffee with friends   sport on TV
> the gym   running   a party (x2)

have
dinner with friends
_____
_____

watch
_____
_____
_____

go
_____
_____

go to
_____
_____
_____

b CD3 ▶55 **PRONUNCIATION** Listen and practise the phrases in **1a**.

c Work with your partner. Write one more word or phrase for the verbs in **1a**.

have breakfast   go to a concert

2 a Write two true sentences and two false sentences about your future plans. Use *be going to* and phrases from **1**.

I'm going to have a party on Saturday.

b Work in pairs. Say your sentences. Guess if your partner's sentences are true or false.

> I'm going to have a party on Saturday.

> I think that's false.

> No, it's true! It's my birthday!

Future plans

3 a CD3 ▶56 Look at the photo and listen to the conversation. What are Rosie, Andy and Jason going to do on Friday?

b Listen again. Answer these questions.

1 When is Rosie going to move to South Africa?
2 What is her husband going to do there?
3 Is Rosie going to look for a job?
4 Where are her brothers going to live?
5 Are Rosie and her husband going to have a party?
6 What is Andy going to do this evening?

HELP WITH GRAMMAR
be going to: questions and short answers

4 a Look at these questions. Notice the word order.

WH- QUESTIONS (?)

When	is	Rosie	**going to**	**move**	to South Africa?
What	is	her husband	**going to**	**do**	there?

b Write these questions in the table.

1 Where **are** her brothers **going to live**?
2 What **is** Andy **going to do** this evening?

c Fill in the gaps with *am, is, are, isn't* and *aren't*.

YES / NO QUESTIONS (?)	SHORT ANSWERS
Are you going to see a film?	Yes, I _____ . No, I'm not.
_____ she going to look for a job?	Yes, she is. No, she _____ .
_____ you going to sell your flat?	Yes, we _____ . No, we aren't.
_____ they going to have a party?	Yes, they are. No, they _____ .

GRAMMAR 10.2 ▶ p133

Andy

Rosie

Jason

Get ready ... Get it right!

6 Write *yes / no* questions with *you* for these plans. Use *be going to* and verbs from **1a**.

- shopping on Saturday?
  Are you going to go shopping on Saturday?
- TV tonight?
- the cinema this week?
- coffee with friends after class?
- swimming or running next weekend?
- the gym next week?
- a party next weekend?
- dinner with friends on Saturday evening?

5 **a** Make questions with these words.

1 are / What / next weekend / going to / you / do ?
   What are you going to do next weekend?
2 after class / are / going to / you / What / do ?
3 going to / you / When / your homework / do / are ?
4 get up / are / going to / you / tomorrow / What time ?
5 you / tomorrow evening / are / Where / dinner / have / going to ?
6 going to / you / next year / go / are / on holiday / Where ?

b **CD3 ▶57** **PRONUNCIATION** Listen and check. Listen again and practise.

What are you going to /tə/ do next weekend?

c Work in pairs. Ask and answer the questions in **5a**. Make notes on your partner's answers.

d Work in new pairs. Talk about your partner in **5c**.

7 **a** Ask other students your questions. Find one person who is going to do each thing. Then ask one more question.

> Are you going to go shopping on Saturday?
>> Yes, I am.
> What are you going to buy?
>> A new dress.

b Tell the class about one student's plans.

> Hiromi's going to buy a new dress on Saturday.

Vocabulary adjectives (3); feelings
Real World saying goodbye and good luck

QUICK REVIEW Phrases with *have, watch, go, go to*
Work in pairs. Write all the phrases with *have, watch, go* and *go to* you can remember (*have a party*, etc.). Then compare phrases with another pair. Who has more phrases?

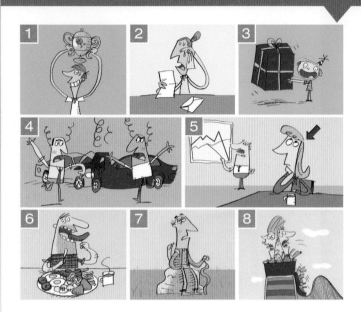

A | *Sally*

Chris

How do you feel?

1 a Work in pairs. Match these adjectives to pictures 1–8. Then check in VOCABULARY 10.4 ▶ p132.

> excited 3 tired ☐ happy ☐ sad ☐
> bored ☐ scared ☐ hungry ☐ angry ☐

TIP • We can say *I'm excited*, etc. or *I feel excited*, etc.

b CD3 ▶ 58 PRONUNCIATION Listen and practise.

c Work in new pairs. Test your partner.

> Who's happy?

> The man in picture 1.

2 a Complete these sentences with *always, usually, sometimes* or *never* to make them true for you.

1 I'm _____ happy on my birthday.
2 I'm _____ bored at the weekend.
3 I'm _____ angry with my friends.
4 I'm _____ tired on Friday evenings.
5 I'm _____ hungry at 4 a.m.
6 I'm _____ excited before I go on holiday.
7 I'm _____ scared when I fly.
8 I'm _____ sad when I say goodbye to people.

b Work in pairs. Compare sentences.

See you soon!

3 a Look at photos A–C. Where are the people?

b VIDEO ▶ 10 CD3 ▶ 59 Close your books. Then watch or listen to the people's conversations. When are they going to see each other again?

4 a Work in pairs. How much can you remember? Choose the correct words in conversations A–C.

A
SALLY Right, it's time to go. That's my ¹*train* / *bus*.
CHRIS OK. See you soon. Have a good ²*journey* / *holiday*.
SALLY Thanks a lot.
CHRIS Text me when you arrive in ³*Manchester* / *London*.
SALLY Yes, of course. See you in ⁴*two* / *three* hours. Bye!

B
DANNY It's ten past ⁵*ten* / *eleven*. Time to go.
KAREN Yes, you're right. I don't want to be late.
DANNY OK. See you ⁶*tomorrow* / *this evening*.
KAREN Have a good ⁷*day* / *journey*.
DANNY You too. And good luck with your ⁸*driving test* / *job interview*.
KAREN Thanks a lot. See you.

C
DOROTA Are you going to study here next ⁹*year* / *course*?
KHALID Yes, I am.
DOROTA Me too. See you in ¹⁰*September* / *December*.
KHALID Yes, see you.
DOROTA And good luck with your new ¹¹*school* / *job*.
KHALID Thanks very much. Goodbye.

b VIDEO ▶ 10 CD3 ▶ 59 Watch or listen again. Check your answers.

B | Danny | Karen

C | Khalid | Dorota

REAL WORLD Saying goodbye and good luck

5   **a**   Fill in the gaps with these words.

~~journey~~   much   lot   job   see   September

| **Have a good** (¹*journey*). | **Thanks a** ²_____ . |

| **See you** (in ³_____). | Yes, ⁴_____ you. |

| **Good luck with your** (new ⁵_____). | Thanks very ⁶_____ . |

b   Work in pairs. Which phrase in **bold** in **5a** can you use with these words or phrases?

holiday   in two hours   driving test
day   this evening   weekend   on Monday
exam   birthday   new school
soon   time   English test   later

Have a good holiday.

REAL WORLD 10.1 ▶ **p133**

6   **CD3** ▶ 60   **PRONUNCIATION**   Listen and practise the sentences in **5**.

Have a good journey.

7   **a**   Put conversations A and B in order.

A

ALAN   Oh, nice. Have a good time.
ALAN   What are you going to do after work?   *1*
ALAN   Thanks very much. See you tomorrow.
JANE   I'm going to have dinner with friends.   *2*
JANE   Yes, see you. Bye!
JANE   Thanks a lot. And good luck with your exam.

B

RYAN   Thanks. Oh, and good luck with your new job.
RYAN   To Edinburgh, in Scotland.
RYAN   I'm going to go on holiday next week.
LILY   Really? Where are you going?
LILY   Thanks a lot.
LILY   Well, have a good holiday.

b   **CD3** ▶ 61   Listen and check.

c   Work in pairs. Practise the conversations in **7a**.

8   **a**   Think of two things you're going to do in the future.

b   Work in groups or with the whole class. Talk about your plans. Use sentences from **5**.

I'm going to visit my sister on Sunday.

Have a good time.

HELP WITH PRONUNCIATION Vowel sounds: review

1 CD3 ▶62 Listen to the sounds and words. Listen again and practise.

/æ/ bag	/ə/ computer	/ɪ/ six	/iː/ nineteen
have			

/ɒ/ coffee	/ʌ/ umbrella	/ɔː/ forty	/ɜː/ burger

2 **a** Work in pairs. Write these words in the table. There are three words for each sound.

~~have~~	keys	different	breakfast	long	girl	market
jeans	bored	country	holiday	amazing	walk	work
angry	hungry	because	university	bought	beach	
ticket	money	fantastic	cinema			

b CD3 ▶63 Listen and check. Listen again and practise.

3 **a** CD3 ▶64 Listen to these sentences. Listen again and practise.

1 In my bag there's some money, an umbrella and my keys.
2 I have a big breakfast before I walk to work at the university.
3 Tom's very angry because he can't find his cinema ticket.
4 They went on a long holiday to forty different countries!
5 The girl was hungry and bored so she had a burger and a coffee.
6 I bought these fantastic jeans at an amazing market near the beach.

b Work in pairs. Take turns to say the sentences.

▶ continue2learn

▶ Vocabulary, Grammar and Real World

- **Extra Practice 10 and Progress Portfolio 10** p106
- **Language Summary 10** p132
- **10A–D** Workbook p48
- **Self-study DVD-ROM 10** with Review Video

▶ Reading and Writing

- **Portfolio 10** Happy birthday! Workbook p70
  Reading greetings cards; a thank-you email
  Writing messages on greetings cards; word order: review; a thank-you email

---

Work in groups of four. Read the rules. Then play the game!

Rules

You need: One counter for each student; one dice for each group.

How to play: Put your counters on **START**. Take turns to throw the dice, move your counter and read the instructions on the square. The first student to get to **FINISH** is the winner.

Grammar and Vocabulary squares: The first student to land on a Grammar or Vocabulary square answers question 1. If the other students think your answer is correct, you can stay on the square. If the answer is wrong, move back to the last square you were on. The second student to land on the same square answers question 2. If a third or fourth student lands on the same square, he or she can stay on the square without answering a question.

Talk about squares: If you land on a Talk about square, talk about the topic for 15 seconds. If you can't talk for 15 seconds, move back to the last square you were on. If a second or third student lands on the same square, he or she also talks about the same topic for 15 seconds.

End of Course Review

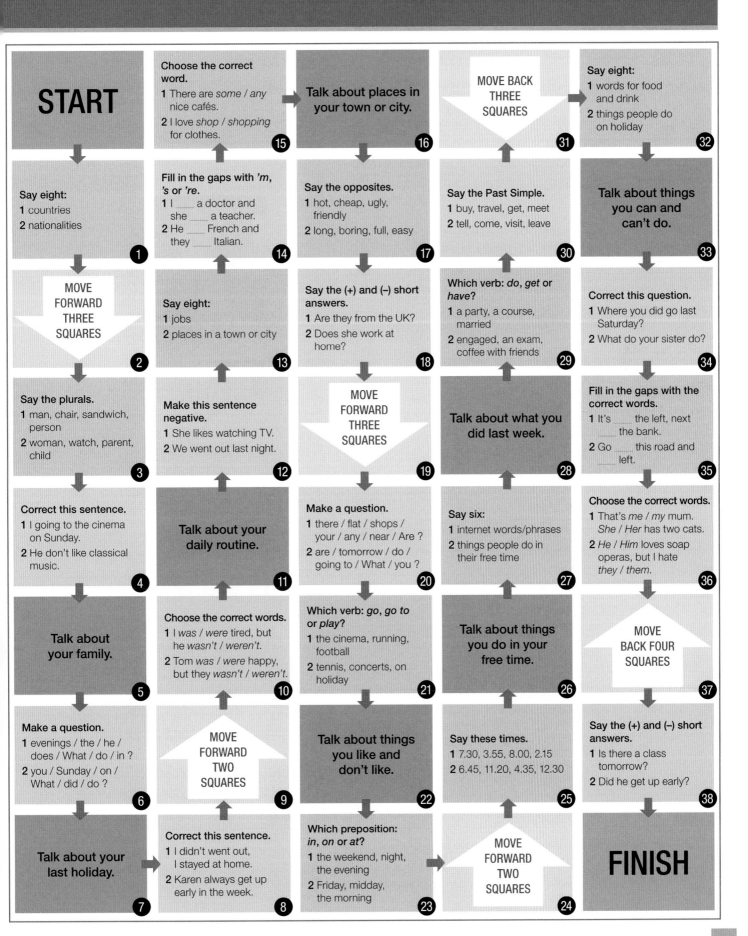

START

Choose the correct word.
1 There are *some* / *any* nice cafés.
2 I love *shop* / *shopping* for clothes.
15

Talk about places in your town or city.
16

MOVE BACK THREE SQUARES
31

Say eight:
1 words for food and drink
2 things people do on holiday
32

Say eight:
1 countries
2 nationalities
1

Fill in the gaps with 'm, 's or 're.
1 I ____ a doctor and she ____ a teacher.
2 He ____ French and they ____ Italian.
14

Say the opposites.
1 hot, cheap, ugly, friendly
2 long, boring, full, easy
17

Say the Past Simple.
1 buy, travel, get, meet
2 tell, come, visit, leave
30

Talk about things you can and can't do.
33

MOVE FORWARD THREE SQUARES
2

Say eight:
1 jobs
2 places in a town or city
13

Say the (+) and (–) short answers.
1 Are they from the UK?
2 Does she work at home?
18

Which verb: *do*, *get* or *have*?
1 a party, a course, married
2 engaged, an exam, coffee with friends
29

Correct this question.
1 Where you did go last Saturday?
2 What do your sister do?
34

Say the plurals.
1 man, chair, sandwich, person
2 woman, watch, parent, child
3

Make this sentence negative.
1 She likes watching TV.
2 We went out last night.
12

MOVE FORWARD THREE SQUARES
19

Talk about what you did last week.
28

Fill in the gaps with the correct words.
1 It's ____ the left, next ____ the bank.
2 Go ____ this road and ____ left.
35

Correct this sentence.
1 I going to the cinema on Sunday.
2 He don't like classical music.
4

Talk about your daily routine.
11

Make a question.
1 there / flat / shops / your / any / near / Are ?
2 are / tomorrow / do / going to / What / you ?
20

Say six:
1 internet words/phrases
2 things people do in their free time
27

Choose the correct words.
1 That's *me* / *my* mum. *She* / *Her* has two cats.
2 *He* / *Him* loves soap operas, but I hate *they* / *them*.
36

Talk about your family.
5

Choose the correct words.
1 I *was* / *were* tired, but he *wasn't* / *weren't*.
2 Tom *was* / *were* happy, but they *wasn't* / *weren't*.
10

Which verb: *go*, *go to* or *play*?
1 the cinema, running, football
2 tennis, concerts, on holiday
21

Talk about things you do in your free time.
26

MOVE BACK FOUR SQUARES
37

Make a question.
1 evenings / the / he / does / What / do / in ?
2 you / Sunday / on / What / did / do ?
6

MOVE FORWARD TWO SQUARES
9

Talk about things you like and don't like.
22

Say these times.
1 7.30, 3.55, 8.00, 2.15
2 6.45, 11.20, 4.35, 12.30
25

Say the (+) and (–) short answers.
1 Is there a class tomorrow?
2 Did he get up early?
38

Talk about your last holiday.
7

Correct this sentence.
1 I didn't went out, I stayed at home.
2 Karen always get up early in the week.
8

Which preposition: *in*, *on* or *at*?
1 the weekend, night, the evening
2 Friday, midday, the morning
23

MOVE FORWARD TWO SQUARES
24

FINISH

Pair and Group Work: Student A

1A 10 p7

a Work on your own. Practise the phone numbers.

	you	your partner
📱	07395 623108	
☎	0161 288 9104	

b Work with your partner. Ask questions with *What's your … ?*. Write your partner's phone numbers in the table.

c Check your partner's table. Are the numbers correct?

4B 9 p33

a Work on your own. Make questions with these words.

1 a lot / you / Do / eat out ?
   Do you eat out a lot?

2 DVDs / watch / you / Do / a lot of ?

3 in / live / you / a house or a flat / Do ?

4 food / like / you / Do / Italian ?

5 you / Do / old / computer / an / have ?

b Work with your partner. Ask your questions in **a**.

c Answer your partner's questions.

6B 7 p49

a Look at these questions about places near Susan's flat. Fill in the gaps with *Is*, *Are*, *a* or *any*. The answers are in brackets ( ).

1 *Is* there *a* post office near Susan's flat? (✓)
2 _____ there _____ good restaurants? (✗)
3 _____ there _____ bus stop? (✓)
4 _____ there _____ museums? (✗)
5 _____ there _____ cashpoint? (✓)

b Work with your partner. Ask your questions from **a**. Are your partner's answers correct?

c Answer your partner's questions. Are your answers correct?

7A 11 p55

a Work on your own. Write questions with *Do you like … ?* for the things in column A of the table.

1 *Do you like horror films?*

A	B (✓ or ✗)	C (✓ or ✗)
1		
2		
3		
4		
5		
6		

b Work on your own. Guess if your partner likes the things in the table. Put a tick (✓) or a cross (✗) in column B of the table.

c Work with your partner. Ask your questions from **a**. Put a tick (✓) or a cross (✗) in column C of the table. Are your guesses correct?

d Answer your partner's questions.

e Tell the class two things about your partner.

> Rafael doesn't like horror films.
> He loves playing video games.

1B p9

a Look at the photo. Ask about people 1, 3 and 5. Write the names and countries.

> Number 1. What's his name?

> Where's he from?

b Answer your partner's questions about people 2, 4 and 6.

c Look at the photo for one minute. Remember the people's names and countries.

d Close your books. Ask and answer questions about the people.

> Where's David from?

> He's from the UK.

1 Name _____
  Country _____

2 Name _David_
  Country _the UK_

3 Name _____
  Country _____

4 Name _Nina_
  Country _Italy_

5 Name _____
  Country _____

6 Name _Polly_
  Country _the USA_

2B p17

a Look at these photos. Write *yes / no* questions to check the information in blue about Roberto, Wendy and Alex.

Is Roberto Spanish?

b Work with your partner. Ask your questions from **a**. Tick (✓) the correct information. Change the wrong information.

c Answer your partner's questions about Silvio, Yi Chen and Omar.

> Is Silvio Italian?

> No, he isn't. He's Brazilian.

d Compare answers with another student A.

> Roberto isn't Spanish. He's Mexican.

name	Roberto	Wendy	Alex
nationality	Spanish?	American?	Russian?
job	a police officer?	a waitress?	a teacher?
married or single	married?	married?	married?

name	Silvio	Yi Chen	Omar
nationality	Brazilian	Chinese	Egyptian
job	a taxi driver	a sales assistant	an actor
married or single	married	married	single

3A 13 p23

Alice and Mike

a Work on your own. Choose the correct words.

1 Where *is / are* Alice and Mike?
2 *Is / Are* the people very friendly?
3 *Is / Are* Alice and Mike in a big hotel?
4 Where *'s / are* the hotel?
5 *Is / Are* the rooms very big?
6 *Is / Are* it very cold?

b Check the answers in email A on p22.

c Work with your partner. Ask your questions about Alice and Mike in **a**. Are your partner's answers correct?

d Answer your partner's questions about Liz and Steve. Don't look at p23!

8B 10 p65

a Work on your own. Fill in the gaps with *was* or *were*.

1 Where __was__ the last wedding you went* to?
2 When _____ it?
3 Who _____ the bride and groom?
4 How many people _____ at the wedding?
5 _____ the food good?
6 _____ any of your friends there?
7 _____ there a party after the wedding?
8 _____ there any music?

*went = Past Simple of *go*

b Work with your partner. Ask your questions from **a**. Make notes on his or her answers.

c Answer your partner's questions about the last party you went to.

d Work with another student A. Tell him or her about the wedding your partner went to.

4C 9 p35

a You are a customer. Your partner is a shop assistant. Buy things a–d from your partner's shop. You start. How much do you spend?

> Excuse me. Do you have any … ?
> How much is this … , please?
> How much are these … , please?
> Can I have … , please?
> No, that's all, thanks.
> Here you are.

b You are a shop assistant. Your partner is a customer. He or she wants to buy things 1–4. Have a conversation with your partner. Your partner starts.

> Yes, they're over there.
> It's £… .
> They're …p each.
> Sure. Anything else?
> OK, that's £… .

4D 8 p36

a Look at these film times. Work with your partner. Take turns to ask the times of the films. Write the times.

> What time is *The Italian Teacher* on?

> It's on at quarter past four, …

FILM TIMES

The Italian Teacher	4.15		
Seven Sisters	2.55	5.15	8.50
Married or Single?		7.20	
Beautiful Day	3.30	5.45	9.05
Monday to Friday	3.05		
The Actor's Wife	3.45	6.50	9.15

b Check the times with your partner. Are they correct?

5A 8 p39

a Work on your own. Fill in the gaps in the questions in column A of the table. Use *Do* and these verbs.

~~get up~~   have   sleep   drink   watch

A	B your partner's answer (✓ or ✗)
1 _Do_ you _get up_ before seven o'clock?	
2 _____ you _____ TV in the morning?	
3 _____ you _____ breakfast in a café?	
4 _____ you _____ a lot of coffee?	
5 _____ you _____ in the day?	

b Work with your partner. Ask questions 1–5. Put a tick (✓) or a cross (✗) in column B of the table.

> Do you get up before seven o'clock?

> Yes, I do. / No, I don't. I get up at about eight.

c Answer your partner's questions. Give more information if possible.

d Work with another student A. Tell him or her about your partner.

> Uli gets up at about eight.

5B 8 p41

a Work on your own. Fill in the gaps in these questions about Nadine's routine. Use *does she* and the correct prepositions.

1 What time _does_ _she_ get up _in_ the week?
2 What _____ _____ do ____ Wednesday afternoon?
3 _____ _____ have classes ____ Friday morning?
4 _____ _____ go out with friends ____ the weekend?
5 _____ _____ phone her mother ____ Sunday evening?

b Work with your partner. Ask your partner the questions in **a**.

c Look at pictures a–e. Then answer your partner's questions.

the week

Wednesday evening

the weekend

Sunday evening

7B 10 p57

a Work on your own. Look at the things Megan and Harry can and can't do. Write questions with *Can* for the **pink** gaps in the table.

1 Can Megan speak German?

	Megan	Harry
1 Guten Tag!		✗
2 (piano)	✓	
3 (guitar)		✓
4 (bicycle)	✓	
5 (skis)		✗
6 (swimming pool)	✓	
7 (tennis)		✗
8 (basketball)	✗	

b Work with your partner. Take turns to ask your questions from **a**. Fill in the gaps in the table with a tick (✓) or a cross (✗). You start.

c Compare tables with your partner. What can both children do?

9B 10 p73

a Work on your own. Make questions about Heidi with the words in column A of the table.

A	B Heidi	C Charlie
1 she / every / What / afternoon / do / did ? *What did she do every afternoon?*		(go) sightseeing
2 museums / visit / she / Did / any ?		✗
3 the evenings / she / do / did / What / in ?		(have) dinner in his hotel
4 she / did / around / How / travel ?		(rent) a car
5 buy / Did / presents / any / she ?		✓

b Work with your partner. Ask your questions from **a** about Heidi. Write the answers in column B of the table.

c Look at column C. Answer your partner's questions about Charlie. Use the Past Simple form of the verbs in brackets.

9C 7 p74

a You are at a station. You want to buy these tickets. Your partner is a ticket seller. Ask your partner questions and complete the table. The time now is 9 a.m.

ticket	price	time of next train	platform	time train arrives
two returns to Bath (you want to come back tomorrow)				
two singles to Bristol				

b You are a ticket seller. Your partner wants to buy some tickets. Look at this information. Answer your partner's questions.

place	price	time of next train	platform	time train arrives
Leeds	single: £28.20 return: £42.50	10.10	2	11.39
Manchester	single: £43.40 return: £55.80	9.25	5	12.41

Pair and Group Work: Student B

1A 🔟 p7

a Work on your own. Practise the phone numbers.

	you	your partner
	07902 715843	
	020 7911 6047	

b Work with your partner. Ask questions with *What's your ... ?*. Write your partner's phone numbers in the table.

c Check your partner's table. Are the numbers correct?

4B 9️⃣ p33

a Work on your own. Make questions with these words.

a watch / you / Do / a lot / TV ?

   Do you watch TV a lot?

b tennis / Do / play / you / or football ?

c an / you / in / work / office / Do ?

d Chinese / like / Do / food / you ?

e mobile / have / phone / a / you / new / Do ?

b Work with your partner. Answer his or her questions.

c Ask your questions in **a**.

6B 7️⃣ p49

a Look at these questions about places near Susan's flat. Fill in the gaps with *Is*, *Are*, *a* or *any*. The answers are in brackets ( ).

1 *Is* there *a* station near Susan's flat? (✗)
2 _____ there _____ shops? (✓)
3 _____ there _____ chemist's? (✓)
4 _____ there _____ nice cafés? (✗)
5 _____ there _____ supermarket? (✓)

b Work with your partner. Answer his or her questions. Are your answers correct?

c Ask your questions from **a**. Are your partner's answers correct?

7A 1️⃣1️⃣ p55

a Work on your own. Write questions with *Do you like ... ?* for the things in column A of the table.

a *Do you like Chinese food?*

A	B (✓ or ✗)	C (✓ or ✗)
a		
b		
c		
d		
e		
f		

b Work on your own. Guess if your partner likes the things in the table. Put a tick (✓) or a cross (✗) in column B of the table.

c Work with your partner. Answer his or her questions.

d Ask your questions from **a**. Put a tick (✓) or a cross (✗) in column C of the table. Are your guesses correct?

e Tell the class two things about your partner.

> Katarina doesn't like Chinese food.
> She loves shopping for clothes.

1B ⑨ p9

a Look at the photo. Answer your partner's questions about people 1, 3 and 5.

b Ask about people 2, 4 and 6. Write the names and countries.

> Number 2. What's his name?

> Where's he from?

c Look at the photo for one minute. Remember the people's names and countries.

d Close your books. Ask and answer questions about the people.

> Where's Sue from?

> She's from Australia.

1 Name _Adam_
   Country _Germany_

2 Name _____
   Country _____

3 Name _Mario_
   Country _Spain_

4 Name _____
   Country _____

5 Name _Sue_
   Country _Australia_

6 Name _____
   Country _____

2B ⑨ p17

a Look at these photos. Write *yes / no* questions to check the information in blue about Silvio, Yi Chen and Omar.

Is Silvio Italian?

b Work with your partner. Answer his or her questions about Roberto, Wendy and Alex.

> Is Roberto Spanish?

> No, he isn't. He's Mexican.

c Ask your partner your questions from **a**. Tick (✓) the correct information. Change the wrong information.

d Compare answers with another student B.

> Silvio isn't Italian. He's Brazilian.

name	Silvio	Yi Chen	Omar
nationality	Italian?	Japanese?	Egyptian?
job	a taxi driver?	a musician?	a doctor?
married or single	married?	married?	married?

name	Roberto	Wendy	Alex
nationality	Mexican	British	Russian
job	a police officer	a waitress	a manager
married or single	single	single	married

3A 13 p23

Liz and Steve

a Work on your own. Choose the correct words.

1 Where *is* / *are* Liz and Steve?
2 *Is* / *Are* the people very friendly?
3 *Is* / *Are* Liz and Steve in a big hotel?
4 Where *'s* / *are* the hotel?
5 *Is* / *Are* the rooms very nice?
6 *Is* / *Are* the hotel cheap?

b Check the answers in email B on p23.

c Work with your partner. Answer your partner's questions about Alice and Mike. Don't look at p22!

d Ask your questions about Liz and Steve in **a**. Are your partner's answers correct?

8B 10 p65

a Work on your own. Fill in the gaps with *was* or *were*.

1 Where ___was___ the last party you went* to?
2 _____ it a friend's party?
3 How many people _____ at the party?
4 _____ any of your family there?
5 When _____ the party?
6 _____ there any interesting people?
7 _____ the music good?
8 _____ there any food?

*went = Past Simple of *go*

b Work with your partner. Answer his or her questions about the last wedding you went to.

c Ask your partner your questions from **a**. Make notes on his or her answers.

d Work with another student B. Tell him or her about the party your partner went to.

4C 9 p35

a You are a shop assistant. Your partner is a customer. He or she wants to buy things a–d. Have a conversation with your partner. Your partner starts.

Yes, they're over there.
It's £… .
They're £… each.
Sure. Anything else?
OK, that's £… .

b You are a customer. Your partner is a shop assistant. Buy things 1–4 from your partner's shop. You start. How much do you spend?

Excuse me. Do you have any … ?
How much is this … , please?
How much are these … , please?
Can I have … , please?
No, that's all, thanks.
Here you are.

4D 8 p36

a Look at these film times. Work with your partner. Take turns to ask the times of the films. Write the times.

> What time is *Seven Sisters* on?

> It's on at five to three, …

FILM TIMES

The Italian Teacher	4.15	7.00	9.25
Seven Sisters	2.55		
Married or Single?	4.25	7.20	9.10
Beautiful Day		5.45	
Monday to Friday	3.05	4.50	6.45
The Actor's Wife			9.15

b Check the times with your partner. Are they correct?

5A 8 p39

a Work on your own. Fill in the gaps in the questions in column A of the table. Use *Do* and these verbs.

> get   eat   work   go   have

A	B your partner's answer (✓ or ✗)
a *Do* you *get* home after six o'clock?	
b _____ you _____ dinner before nine?	
c _____ you _____ to bed after midnight?	
d _____ you _____ at the weekend?	
e _____ you _____ a lot of fruit?	

b Work with your partner. Answer his or her questions. Give more information if possible.

c Ask your partner questions a–e. Put a tick (✓) or a cross (✗) in column B of the table.

> Do you get home after six o'clock?

> Yes, I do. / No, I don't. I get home at about five.

d Work with another student B. Tell him or her about your partner.

> Kwan gets home at about five.

5B 8 p41

a Work on your own. Fill in the gaps in these questions about Nadine's routine. Use *does she* and the correct prepositions.

1 What time *does she* go to bed *in* the week?

2 _____ _____ have classes ___ Tuesday morning?

3 What _____ _____ do ___ Wednesday evening?

4 What time _____ _____ get up ___ the weekend?

5 _____ _____ eat out ___ Sunday evening?

b Work with your partner. Look at pictures a–e. Then answer your partner's questions.

c Ask your partner the questions in **a**.

the week

Wednesday afternoon

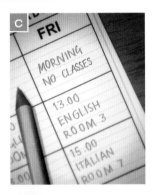

the weekend

Sunday evening

7B 10 p57

a Work on your own. Look at the things Megan and Harry can and can't do. Write questions with *Can* for the **pink** gaps in the table.

1 Can Harry speak German?

	Megan	Harry
1 Guten Tag!	✓	
2		✗
3	✗	
4		✓
5	✗	
6		✓
7	✓	
8		✗

b Work with your partner. Take turns to ask your questions from **a**. Fill in the gaps in the table with a tick (✓) or a cross (✗). Your partner starts.

c Compare tables with your partner. What can both children do?

9B 10 p73

a Work on your own. Make questions about Charlie with the words in column A of the table.

A	B Charlie	C Heidi
1 he / every / What / morning / do / did ? *What did he do every morning?*		(go) for a walk
2 museums / visit / he / Did / any ?		✓
3 the evenings / he / do / did / What / in ?		(have) dinner with her friends
4 he / around / did / travel / How ?		(go) by bus and taxi
5 buy / Did / presents / any / he ?		✗

b Work with your partner. Look at column C. Answer his or her questions about Heidi. Use the Past Simple form of the verbs in brackets.

c Ask your partner your questions from **a** about Charlie. Write the answers in column B of the table.

9C 7 p74

a You are at a station. You are a ticket seller. Your partner wants to buy some tickets. Look at this information. Answer your partner's questions. The time now is 9 a.m.

place	price	time of next train	platform	time train arrives
Bath	single: £29.50 return: £39.70	9.15	8	10.39
Bristol	single: £36.30 return: £45.50	10.19	6	11.55

b You want to buy these tickets. Your partner is a ticket seller. Ask your partner questions and complete the table.

ticket	price	time of next train	platform	time train arrives
two returns to Leeds (you want to come back next weekend)				
two singles to Manchester				

Pair and Group Work: Other activities

1D 7 p12

a Work with your partner. Look at the picture. Write the words and the number of people and things.

5	ch _a_ _i_ _r_ _s_
	ta _ _ _ _ _
	me _ _
	wo _ _ _ _
	bo _ _ _ _
	pe _ _ _
	pe _ _ _ _ _
	ap _ _ _ _
	ba _ _ _
	mo _ _ _

b Work with another pair. Compare answers.

c Check on p134. Are your answers correct?

8A 6 p63

a Work on your own. Think about your life when you were ten. Write six sentences about you with *was* or *were*. Use these ideas or your own.

> **When I was ten,**
> * my favourite singer / band …
> * my favourite food / drink …
> * my favourite TV programme(s) …
> * my favourite film(s) …
> * I … happy / unhappy at school.
> * I … good at (sports, languages …).
> * I … always / usually / never late for class.
> * my brother(s) / sister(s) … nice to me.

b Work with your group. Say your sentences. Are any of the other students' sentences true for you?

> When I was ten, my favourite band was U2.

> Me too!

c Tell the class two interesting things about other students in your group.

9A 9 p71

a Work on your own. Think about the last time you visited a different town or city. Write 6–8 sentences. Use these phrases and your own ideas.

* I (go) to …
  I went to Buenos Aires two months ago.
* I (go) there by …
* I (arrive) at … o'clock.
* I (travel) on my own / with my …
* When I was there I (visit) …
* I also (go) to …
* I (go) shopping and I (buy) …
* I (leave) there … and (get) home …
* I (be) there for … days / weeks.
* I (have) a good / great / terrible time.

b Work on your own. Practise your sentences until you can remember them.

c Work with your group. Tell each other about the last time you visited a different town or city.

d Tell the class two things about the place you visited.

Extra Practice 1

Language Summary 1 p114

1A p6

1 Choose the correct words.

A Hello, [1](*I*)/ *my* 'm Andy. What's
[2]*you* / *your* name?

B Hello, [3]*I* / *my* name's Kara.

A Nice to meet [4]*you* / *your*.

B [5]*You* / *Your* too.

A Hello, Caroline.

B Hi, Pia. How are [6]*you* / *your*?

A [7]*I* / *My* 'm fine, thanks. And
[8]*you* / *your*?

B [9]*I* / *My* 'm OK, thanks.

A What's [10]*you* / *your* mobile
number?

B It's 07700 900349.

A Thanks. And what's [11]*you* / *your*
home number?

B It's 020 7946 0682.

A Goodbye, Pia.

B Bye, Jo. See [12]*you* / *your* soon.

A Yes, see [13]*you* / *your*.

2 Write the numbers.

0 *z e r o*   7 s _ _ _ _ _

1 o _ _   8 e _ _ _ _

2 t _ _   9 n _ _ _ _

3 t _ _ _ _   10 t _ _

4 f _ _ _   11 e _ _ _ _ _

5 f _ _ _   12 t _ _ _ _ _

6 s _ _

1B p8

3 Write the letters in countries 1–9.
Find the country (↓).

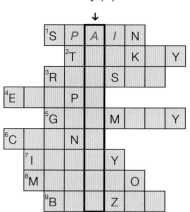

4 Fill in the gaps with *he*, *his*, *she* or *her*.

A What's [1] *his* name?

B [2]_____ name's Johnny.

A Where's [3]_____ from?

B [4]_____ 's from the UK.

A What's [5]_____ name?

B [6]_____ name's Anna.

A Where's [7]_____ from?

B [8]_____ 's from the USA.

1C p10

5 Write the vowels (*a*, *e*, *i*, *o*, *u*) in
these things. Then choose *a* or
an.

1 (a)/ **an** b a g

2 **a** / **an** _ ppl _

3 **a** / **an** d _ ct _ _ n _ ry

4 **a** / **an** n _ t _ b _ _ k

5 **a** / **an** b _ _ k

6 **a** / **an** _ mbr _ ll _

7 **a** / **an** p _ nc _ l

8 **a** / **an** p _ n

9 **a** / **an** m _ b _ l _

6 Make questions and sentences with these words.

1 surname / your / What's ?
   What's your surname?

2 your / name / What's / first ?
   _____

3 that / you / How / spell / do ?
   _____

4 bag / mean / does / What ?
   _____

5 English / this / in / What's ?
   _____

6 know / don't / sorry, / I / I'm .
   _____

7 you / Egypt / do / spell / How ?
   _____

8 repeat / please / you / that, /
   Can ?
   _____

9 understand / don't / sorry, /
   I / I'm .
   _____

1D p12

7 **a** Find 12 people or things (→↓).

W	O	V	B	O	Y	N	W
D	F	M	A	N	C	E	A
E	D	L	B	B	H	J	T
S	I	A	Y	G	A	R	C
S	A	N	D	W	I	C	H
H	R	G	A	W	R	A	K
J	Y	G	I	R	L	M	D
C	O	M	P	U	T	E	R
P	T	A	B	L	E	R	Z
I	E	L	W	O	M	A	N

b Write the plurals of the words
in **7a**.

boys   _____

_____ _____

_____ _____

_____ _____

_____

Progress Portfolio 1

Tick (✓) the things you can do
in English.

☐ I can say hello and goodbye.

☐ I can ask people's names.

☐ I can introduce people.

☐ I can say phone numbers.

☐ I can ask and say where people
are from.

☐ I can say the alphabet.

☐ I can ask questions in class.

☐ I can say when I don't
understand.

☐ I can ask people to repeat
things.

☐ I can use plurals.

What do you need to
study again? See
Self-study DVD-ROM 1.

Extra Practice 2

2A p14

1 Write the nationalities.

1	Australia	*Australian*
2	Mexico	
3	Italy	
4	the UK	
5	China	
6	Brazil	
7	the USA	
8	Egypt	
9	Spain	
10	Turkey	
11	Russia	
12	Germany	

2 Choose the correct words.

1 Libby *aren't* / *isn't* from the USA, she *'re* / *'s* from the UK.

2 You *aren't* / *isn't* in this class. You *'m* / *'re* in room D.

3 Ross *aren't* / *isn't* his first name, it *'re* / *'s* his surname.

4 I *'m not* / *isn't* from Mexico, I *'m* / *'re* from Colombia.

5 She *'re* / *'s* a Spanish teacher, but she *aren't* / *isn't* from Spain.

2B p16

3 Write the jobs. Use *a* or *an*.

1	*a teacher*	6	
2		7	
3		8	
4		9	
5			

2C p18

6 Write questions with *your* for these answers.

A 1 *What's your first name?*
B It's Eve.
A 2 _____
B Smith.
A 3 _____
B I'm British.
A 4 _____
B It's 12 Lee Road, London.
A 5 _____
B It's 07700 900195.
A 6 _____
B It's e.smith@webnet.com.

4 Make questions with these words.

1 name / your / 's / What ?
 What's your name?

2 you / Where / from / are ?
 _____

3 's / What / job / your ?
 _____

4 from / 's / Where / he ?
 _____

5 job / What / his / 's ?
 _____

6 What / name / 's / her ?
 _____

7 's / job / What / her ?
 _____

5 **a** Fill in the gaps with *Am*, *Are* or *Is*.

1 *Am* I in this room?
2 _____ he a manager?
3 _____ you a student?
4 _____ I in this class?
5 _____ you from the UK?
6 _____ she a teacher?

b Write the short answers to the questions in **5a**.

1 ✓ Yes, *you are* .
2 ✗ No, _____ .
3 ✓ _____ .
4 ✗ _____ .
5 ✗ _____ .
6 ✓ _____ .

2D p20

7 Write the numbers.

13 t h i r t e e n
14 f _ _ _ _ _ _ n
15 f _ _ _ _ _ n
16 s _ _ _ _ _ n
17 s _ _ _ _ _ _ n
18 e _ _ _ _ _ n
19 n _ _ _ _ _ _ n
21 t _ _ _ _ _ - o _ _
33 t _ _ _ _ _ - t _ _
47 f _ _ _ - s _ _ _ _
56 f _ _ _ _ - s _ _
64 s _ _ _ _ - f _ _ _
72 s _ _ _ _ _ - t _ _
89 e _ _ _ _ - n _ _ _
95 n _ _ _ _ - f _ _ _
100 a h _ _ _ _ _ _

8 Fill in the gaps with *'m*, *'s*, *is* or *are*.

A How old [1] *is* your computer?
B It[2]_____ three years old.

A How old [3] _____ she?
B She[4]_____ 23.

A How old [5] _____ you?
B I[6]_____ 31.

Extra Practice 3

Language Summary 3 p118

3A p22

1 Write the adjectives. Then write their opposites.

1	wne	n *ew*	o *ld*
2	lamsl	s_____	b_____
3	docl	c_____	h_____
4	ygul	u_____	b_____
5	paceh	c_____	e_____
6	dogo	g_____	b_____

2 Fill in the gaps with *are*, *'re*, *is*, *'s*, *isn't* or *aren't*.

Hi Ivan

Eva and I ¹ *are* (+) at an English school in London! It² _____ (+) a good school, but it ³ _____ (−) cheap. The teacher, Ann, ⁴ _____ (+) very good and the students ⁵ _____ (+) friendly. We⁶ _____ (+) in a hotel near the school. The rooms ⁷ _____ (+) nice, but they ⁸ _____ (−) very big!

Love Olga

3 **a** Make questions with these words.

1 are / Eva and Olga / Where ?
 Where are Eva and Olga?

2 the / cheap / Is / school ?
 _____

3 teacher / good / the / Is / very ?
 _____

4 the / Are / friendly / students ?
 _____

5 's / hotel / Where / the ?
 _____

6 the / big / Are / rooms / very ?
 _____

b Read the email in **2** again. Answer the questions in **3a**.

1 *They're in London.*
2 _____
3 _____
4 _____
5 _____
6 _____

3B p24

4 Read about Tony's family. Then fill in the gaps with the correct family words.

I'm Tony and my wife's name is Ella. Our son's name is Jim and he's married to Sarah. Their children are Mia and Bob.

1 Bob is Mia's _*brother*_ .
2 Mia is Bob's _____ .
3 Tony is Mia's _____ .
4 Jim is Bob's _____ .
5 Sarah is Mia's _____ .
6 Ella is Bob's _____ .
7 Bob is Sarah's _____ .
8 Tony is Ella's _____ .
9 Mia is Jim's _____ .
10 Jim and Sarah are Mia and Bob's _____ .

5 Choose the correct words.

1 What's *you* / *your* name?
2 This is *he* / *his* mobile.
3 What is *they* / *their* surname?
4 *She* / *Her* is I / *my* teacher.
5 Is *he* / *him* from Germany?
6 This is *we* / *our* house.
7 Are *they* / *their* in your hotel?
8 *We* / *Our* aren't in *he* / *his* English class.

3C p26

6 Read this conversation in a café. Complete the words.

A Can I ¹h *e l p* you?
C Yes, a ²c ___ f ___ and a cheese ³s ___ w ____ , please.
A ⁴E ___ in or ⁵t ____ away?
C ⁶T ____ away, please.
A Sure. Anything ⁷e ____ ?
C No, that's ⁸a ___ , thanks.
A OK, that's £3.20, please.
C ⁹T ____ you very ¹⁰m ____ .
A You're ¹¹w ___ l ____ e.

3D p28

7 **a** Write the food and drink words.

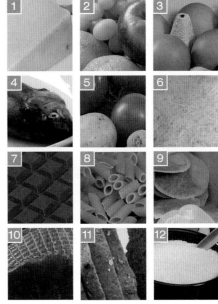

1	c *heese*		7	c_____
2	f_____		8	p_____
3	e_____		9	t_____
4	f_____		10	m_____
5	v_____		11	b_____
6	r_____		12	s_____

b Look at the photo on p28. Check your answers.

Progress Portfolio 3

Tick (✓) the things you can do in English.

☐ I can use adjectives and *very*.
☐ I can understand a simple email.
☐ I can talk about families.
☐ I can talk about money and prices.
☐ I can understand a simple price list.
☐ I can buy food and drink in a café.
☐ I can talk about food and drink I like.

What do you need to study again? See Self-study DVD-ROM 3.

Extra Practice 4

4A p30

1 Choose the correct verbs.

1 (*like*) / *work* football
2 *study* / *live* English
3 *like* / *work* in an office
4 *have* / *study* two children
5 *work* / *like* rock music
6 *study* / *live* languages
7 *have* / *live* in a flat
8 *have* / *work* a car
9 *live* / *have* in the centre of the city
10 *work* / *like* for an Italian company

2 Make these sentences negative.

1 You're a teacher.
   You aren't a teacher.
2 You like Mexican food.
   _____
3 I have a new phone.
   _____
4 I'm from the USA.
   _____
5 We're musicians.
   _____
6 We live in Australia.
   _____
7 Tim and Joe are brothers.
   _____
8 They work in London.
   _____
9 She's a sales assistant.
   _____

4B p32

3 Match the verbs in A to the words and phrases in B.

A	B
go to	DVDs
go	concerts
watch	shopping
play	TV
eat	video games
watch	out
go to	tennis
go	the cinema
play	out with friends

4 Make questions with these words.

1 do / work / Where / you ?
   Where do you work?
2 to / Do / concerts / go / you ?
   _____
3 do / music / they / like / What ?
   _____
4 do / you / live / Where ?
   _____
5 watch / they / Do / TV / a lot ?
   _____
6 you / food / like / Do / Chinese ?
   _____
7 have / we / today / a class / Do ?
   _____
8 do / free time / your / do / What / you / in ?
   _____

4C p34

5 Write the letters in these things in a shop.

1 a p_o_st_c_a_rd
2 a m _ p
3 sw _ _ _ ts
4 b _ tt _ _ ies
5 a m _ g _ z _ _ e
6 a b _ _ _ th _ _ y c _ _ d
7 ch _ w _ _ g g _ m
8 t _ ss _ es
9 a b _ x of ch _ c _ l _ _ es

6 Read this conversation in a shop. Choose the correct words.

C Excuse ¹*you* / (*me*) . ²*Do* / *Are* you have any postcards?
A Yes, ³*their* / *they're* over there.
C OK, thanks. How much ⁴*is* / *are* they?
A ⁵*They're* / *There* 70p each.
C Can I have ⁶*these* / *that* four postcards, please?
A Sure. Anything ⁷*each* / *else* ?
C Yes, ⁸*this* / *those* newspaper.
A OK, ⁹*that* / *that's* £3.80.
C ¹⁰*Here* / *Where* you are.
A ¹¹*Thanks* / *Thank* very much. Goodbye.

4D p36

7 Write the days of the week. Then put them in order 1–7.

oMydna	*Monday 1*
uynSda	_____
dhrsTayu	_____
aStuyadr	_____
ydraiF	_____
seuyTad	_____
daWenydes	_____

8 Write the times.

a   *ten past* three
b   _____ four
c   _____ seven
d   _____ one
e   _____ five
f   _____

Progress Portfolio

Tick (✓) the things you can do in English.

☐ I can talk about things I have and don't have.
☐ I can say where I live and work.
☐ I can talk about my free time.
☐ I can ask people about their free time.
☐ I can buy things in a shop.
☐ I can say the days of the week.
☐ I can tell the time.

What do you need to study again? See Self-study DVD-ROM 4.

Extra Practice 5

5A p38

1 Read these sentences about a typical day. Complete the verbs.

1 I g _e_ _t_ up at 7.00 in the week.
2 I h _ _ _ _ breakfast at 7.30.
3 I l _ _ _ _ home at 8.30.
4 I s _ _ _ _ work at 9.00.
5 I h _ _ _ lunch at 1.00.
6 I f _ _ _ _ _ _ work at 5.30.
7 I g _ _ _ home at 6.00.
8 I h _ _ _ _ dinner at 8.00.
9 I g _ _ to bed at midnight.
10 I s _ _ _ _ _ for seven hours.

2 Put the verbs in the Present Simple.

My best friend's name ¹ _is_ (be) Rob and he ² _____ (live) in London. He ³ _____ (work) in a hotel, but he ⁴ _____ (not like) his job very much. In his free time he ⁵ _____ (go) to the cinema and ⁶ _____ (watch) football on TV a lot. He also ⁷ _____ (study) Spanish on Wednesdays. He ⁸ _____ (have) a very beautiful flat, but he ⁹ _____ (not have) a car. Rob and I ¹⁰ _____ (talk) a lot on the phone, but I ¹¹ _____ (not see) him very much because he ¹² _____ (work) at the weekend.

5B p40

3 Choose the correct words.

1 (on)/ at Thursday
2 in / at the morning
3 on / in Thursday morning
4 in / at night
5 on / in the afternoon
6 in / at the weekend
7 in / at the week
8 at / on midday
9 on / in the evening
10 on / in Sunday evening
11 in / at midnight
12 at / on half past six

4 Fill in the gaps with *does* or *do*.

1 What music _does_ your son like?
2 Where _____ he work?
3 When _____ you start work?
4 What _____ your sister do?
5 When _____ Mike get home?
6 Where _____ Jo and Ed live?
7 What time _____ you get up?

5 **a** Make questions with these words.

1 Alice / cheese / eat / Does ?
   Does Alice eat cheese?
2 fish / like / your / Does / sister ?
   _____
3 concerts / Do / go / they / to ?
   _____
4 in / work / he / Does / a shop ?
   _____
5 have / Does / dad / a car / your ?
   _____
6 like / rock / you / music / Do ?
   _____

b Write short answers to the questions in **5a**.

1 ✓ Yes, _she does_ .
2 ✗ No, _____ .
3 ✗ _____ .
4 ✓ _____ .
5 ✗ _____ .
6 ✓ _____ .

5C p42

6 Read these conversations in a restaurant. Complete the words.

W Hello. Are you ¹r _e_ _a_ _d_ _y_ to ²o _ _ _ _ ?
C Yes. Can I ³h _ _ _ the vegetable lasagne, please?
W Certainly. What ⁴w _ _ _ _ _ you like to ⁵d _ _ _ _ ?
C An orange ⁶j _ _ _ _ _ , please.
W ⁷W _ _ _ _ _ you like a ⁸d _ _ _ _ _ t ?
C Yes, the ⁹s _ _ _ _ b _ _ _ _ y ice cream, please.
W Of ¹⁰c _ _ _ _ _ e .
C Thank you.

7 Write the food and drink words.

1 b _urger_ and c _____
2 m _____ p _____
3 c _____ s _____
4 f _____ s _____
5 a _____ p _____ and c _____
6 b _____ of m _____ w _____

5D p44

8 Tick (✓) the correct sentences. Change the wrong sentences.

1 I'm late for class ⟨never⟩.
2 They eat out every weekend. ✓
3 Lisa's brother always is busy.
4 My dad gets up usually early.
5 She goes to LA every year.
6 We every week go shopping.
7 I sometimes work on Sundays.

Progress Portfolio 5

Tick (✓) the things you can do in English.

☐ I can talk about my routine and other people's routines.
☐ I can use time phrases.
☐ I can ask about other people's routines and free time.
☐ I can understand a simple menu.
☐ I can order food and drink in a restaurant.
☐ I can use frequency adverbs.

What do you need to study again? See Self-study DVD-ROM 5.

Extra Practice 6

6A p46

1 Write the letters in these places in a town or city.

1 a p_a_r k
2 a sho _ p _ _ g c _ nt _ e
3 a t _ _ at _ e
4 a s _ at _ _ n
5 a r _ v _ _
6 an a _ rp _ _ t
7 a b _ _ ld _ _ g
8 a b _ s _ s _ at _ _ n
9 a m _ s _ _ m

2 Choose the correct words.

1 There 's / (are) a lot of old buildings in Bath.
2 There 's / are a station.
3 There are a / a lot of hotels.
4 There 's / are five theatres.
5 There are some / a nice parks.
6 There are a lot of / a cafés.
7 There 's / are a shopping centre.
8 There's an / some airport in Bristol.

6B p48

3 Write the places in a town or city.

1 dora	r _oad_
2 sub spot	b_____ s
3 kabn	b_____
4 kemtar	m_____
5 repsukemtar	s_____
6 stop focife	p_____ o_____
7 rasque	s_____
8 'sithcmes	c_____

4 Read about Ian's home town. Fill in the gaps with 's, are, isn't or aren't.

Ian lives in Barton, in the UK. There ¹ _are_ some good shops in Barton, but there ² _____ a supermarket. There ³ _____ also a nice park, but there ⁴ _____ any old buildings. In Ian's road there's a post office, but there ⁵ _____ a bank. There ⁶ _____ also two cafés near his house, but there ⁷ _____ any restaurants.

5 a Fill in the gaps with Is, Are, a or any.

1 _Are_ there _any_ shops in Barton?
2 _____ there _____ supermarket?
3 _____ there _____ old buildings?
4 _____ there _____ bank in Ian's road?
5 _____ there _____ restaurants near Ian's house?
6 _____ there _____ post office in Ian's road?
7 _____ there _____ cafés near Ian's house?

b Read about Barton in **4** again. Then write the short answers to the questions in **5a**.

1 _Yes, there are._
2 _____ .
3 _____ .
4 _____ .
5 _____ .
6 _____ .
7 _____ .

6C p50

6 Read this conversation at Bath tourist information centre. Fill in the gaps with these phrases.

~~can I~~	When is	minutes away
we book	per person	show me
Do you have	where's	It's open

A Hello, ¹ _can I_ help you?
T Yes, please. ² _____ a map of Bath?
A Yes, of course. Here you are.
T Thank you. And ³ _____ the Thermae Bath Spa?
A It's in Hot Bath Street.
T Can you ⁴ _____ on this map?
A Yes, here it is. It's about ten ⁵ _____ .
T Thanks. ⁶ _____ it open?
A ⁷ _____ from 9 a.m. to 9.30 p.m. every day.
T And can ⁸ _____ a walking tour here?
A Yes, you can. They're £10 ⁹ _____ .

7 Write the words for these things.

1	_a camera_	5	_____
2	_____	6	_____
3	_____	7	_____
4	_____	8	_____

6D p52

8 Find 14 words for clothes (→↓).

J	A	C	K	E	T	S	C
E	T	V	O	Q	R	K	O
A	S	U	I	T	A	I	A
N	Z	T	S	H	I	R	T
S	D	B	J	E	N	T	L
T	R	O	U	S	E	R	S
E	E	O	M	X	R	B	H
K	S	T	P	O	S	U	O
G	S	S	E	M	T	I	E
S	H	I	R	T	F	N	S

Progress Portfolio

Tick (✓) the things you can do in English.

☐ I can talk about places in my town or city.
☐ I can ask about places in other towns or cities.
☐ I can say what is in my bag.
☐ I can ask for information at a tourist information centre.
☐ I can talk about clothes and colours.
☐ I can talk about my favourite things and people.

What do you need to study again? See Self-study DVD-ROM 6.

Extra Practice 7

7A p54

1 Write the letters in these things people like or don't like.

1 s o a p o p er a s
2 ani __ a __ s
3 ho __ __ or fi __ __ s
4 da __ ci __ g
5 f __ y __ n __
6 cla __ ic __ l mu __ i __
7 wa __ c __ ing sp __ __ t on __ V
8 vi __ it __ ng n __ w pl __ __ es
9 s __ __ o __ pi __ g f __ r clo __ __ es

2 Fill in the gaps with these verbs.

> ~~like~~   likes   love   loves
> hate   hates   don't like
> doesn't like

1 😊 I _like_ watching TV.
2 ☹ I _____ tennis.
3 😐 Colin _____ rice.
4 😠 He _____ pizza.
5 🙂 Jo _____ eating out.
6 😠 We _____ football.
7 😊 She _____ coffee.
8 😋 I _____ ice cream.

3 Choose the correct words.

1 Where are (they) / them?
2 She / Her doesn't know we / us.
3 Does he / him like I / me?
4 I / me live with she / her.
5 We / Us never see they / them.
6 Do you work with he / him?

7B p56

4 Tick (✓) the correct sentences. Change the wrong sentences.

1 Their children can't ~~to~~ swim.
2 My mum can speak French. ✓
3 He can't speaks Japanese.
4 I can't understand it.
5 Do you can play tennis?
6 Lydia can dance very good.
7 I can't go to work today.
8 Can you use a computer?
9 Paul can play well football.

5 Look at the pictures. Write sentences with *can*.

1 He _can speak Spanish._
2 She _____ .
3 She _____ .
4 He _____ .
5 She _____ .
6 He _____ .
7 They _____ .
8 She _____ .
9 He _____ .

7C p58

6 Complete the words in these conversations.

A [1]E x c u s e me. [2]W _ _ _ _ _ 's the Queen's Hotel?

B Go [3]a _ _ _ _ _ this road and turn [4]r _ _ _ _ . That's Park Road. The Queen's Hotel is on your [5]l _ _ _ , [6]o _ _ _ _ _ _ e the theatre.

A Thank you very much.

B You're [7]w _ _ _ _ _ e .

A Excuse me. Is there a supermarket [8]n _ _ _ _ here?

B Yes, there is. Go [9]a _ _ _ _ _ this road and turn [10]l _ _ _ . The supermarket is on your [11]r _ _ _ _ , [12]n _ _ _ _ to the chemist's.

A Thanks very much. Oh, and [13]w _ _ _ _ _ 's the post office?

B It's [14]o _ _ _ there, [15]n _ _ _ the bank.

A Oh, yes. I [16]c _ _ see it. Thanks a lot.

7D p60

7 Read about how Vanessa uses the internet. Fill the gaps with these verbs.

> ~~send~~   download   chat
> receive   write   search
> book   sell   listen   watch
> watching   reading

I [1] _send_ and [2]_____ a lot of emails every day and I [3]_____ a blog called 'Vanessa's Life' – all of my friends like [4]_____ it. I use the internet to [5]_____ for information, of course, and I always [6]_____ hotels and flights online. I [7]_____ TV programmes on my laptop and I love [8]_____ videos on YouTube. I also [9]_____ music onto my phone and then I [10]_____ to it on the train. I [11]_____ to my sister online a lot – she lives in Australia – and I also buy and [12]_____ DVDs online. Yes, I love the internet!

Progress Portfolio 7

Tick (✓) the things you can do in English.

☐ I can talk about things I like and don't like.
☐ I can ask about things other people like and don't like.
☐ I can say things I can and can't do.
☐ I can ask what other people can do.
☐ I can ask for, give and understand simple directions.
☐ I can understand a simple interview.
☐ I can talk about things I do online.

What do you need to study again? See Self-study DVD-ROM 7.

Extra Practice 8

8A p62

1 Write the letters in adjectives 1–11. Find the adjective (↓).

```
      ↓
 ¹B O R I N G
 ²Y   U   G
 ³E       Y
        ⁴     S Y
     ⁵W     O     G
      ⁶G         T
 ⁷F   N         T   C
  ⁸S       R
 ⁹T     R     B   E
        ¹⁰L       G
         ¹¹R       T
```

2 Choose the correct words.

1 My dad (was) / were a doctor.
2 These shoes wasn't / weren't very expensive. They was / were only £20.
3 I wasn't / weren't at home on Sunday, I was / were at work.
4 My grandparents was / were from Italy.
5 That wasn't / weren't a very good film.
6 I'm sorry we wasn't / weren't at your birthday party. We was / were in France.
7 We was / were in Germany last week, but the weather wasn't / weren't very good.

8B p64

3 a Fill in the gaps with last, yesterday, in or ago.

Edward was …

a at work an hour _ago_ .
b in Los Angeles _____ week.
c at a party _____ evening.
d in Sydney two years _____ .
e at university _____ 2007.
f in India a month _____ .
g born _____ 1988.
h in Brazil _____ Sunday.

b Put sentences a–h in order.

1a, 2c, …

---

4 Make questions with these words.

1 born / Where / you / were ?
  Where were you born?
2 your / was / born / son / Where ?
  _____
3 were / on your / you / Where / last birthday ?
  _____
4 first / English / was / teacher / your / Who ?
  _____
5 was / class / When / English / first / your ?
  _____
6 were / three / you / ago / years / Where ?
  _____

5 Fill in the gaps with Was or Were. Then write the short answers.

1 A _Were_ you at home last night?
  B ✓ _Yes, I was._
2 A _____ Nick's mother British?
  B ✗ No, _____ .
3 A _____ the concert good?
  B ✓ _____ .
4 A _____ your sons at the party?
  B ✗ _____ .
5 A _____ Alice's brother there?
  B ✓ _____ .
6 A _____ you at work yesterday?
  B ✗ _____ .

8C p66

6 Fill in the gaps with these words.

What	Why	Where
good	think	meet
let's	shall	past

A ¹ _What_ shall we do on Sunday?
B ² _____ don't we play tennis?
A No, I don't ³ _____ so.
B OK, ⁴ _____ go to the park.
A Yes, that's a ⁵ _____ idea. ⁶ _____ shall we meet?
B Let's ⁷ _____ at the café.
A What time ⁸ _____ we meet?
B About half ⁹ _____ two.
A OK. See you then!

---

7 Write the dates.

7th	_seventh_	15th	_____
1st	_____	12th	_____
5th	_____	19th	_____
9th	_____	20th	_____
2nd	_____	26th	_____
3rd	_____	30th	_____
10th	_____	31st	_____

8D p68

8 Write the numbers.

a a thousand _1,000_
b a million _____
c six hundred and seventy-three _____
d four thousand, five hundred _____
e nine hundred and forty-seven _____
f seven hundred and fifty thousand _____
g fifty million _____
h ninety-nine thousand, nine hundred and ninety _____

▶ Progress Portfolio 8

Tick (✓) the things you can do in English.

☐ I can make sentences and ask questions with was and were.
☐ I can say and understand years and past time phrases.
☐ I can say and ask about months and dates.
☐ I can make and respond to suggestions.
☐ I can say and understand big numbers.
☐ I can understand a simple magazine article.

What do you need to study again? See Self-study DVD-ROM 8.

Extra Practice 9

9A p70

1 Write the words for transport.

1 _a taxi_   **5** _____
2 _____   **6** _____
3 _____   **7** _____
4 _____   **8** _____

2 a Write the Past Simple of these verbs. Which verbs are regular?

get up _got up_   start _____
leave _____   buy _____
watch _____   meet _____
have _____   play _____
write _____   go _____

b Fill in the gaps with the Past Simple of the verbs in **2a**.

Yesterday …

1 I _got up_ at 7 a.m.
2 I _____ home at 8 a.m.
3 I _____ work at 9 a.m.
4 I _____ pasta for lunch.
5 I _____ some new clothes.
6 I _____ a friend after work.
7 I _____ TV in the evening.
8 I _____ video games.
9 I _____ some emails.
10 I _____ to bed.

9B p72

3 Match the verbs in A to the words and phrases in B.

A	B
go	a car
rent	on holiday
stay	photos
take	swimming
go	in a hotel
go for	the beach
go to	with friends
stay	sightseeing
go	around
travel	a walk

4 Make these sentences negative.

1 I went out last night.
I didn't go out last night.
2 She told me her surname.
_____
3 I was at school yesterday.
_____
4 He came home last night.
_____
5 We were in Poland in 2012.
_____
6 They liked the food.
_____

5 Fill in the gaps with _did_, _didn't_, _was_, _wasn't_, _were_ or _weren't_.

A What ^{1} _did_ you do last weekend?
B I went to Lara's birthday party.
A ^{2}_____ you have a good time?
B Yes, I ^{3}_____ . It ^{4}_____ a very good party.
A ^{5}_____ Sue at the party?
B No, she ^{6}_____ . But her two brothers ^{7}_____ there.
A OK. And ^{8}_____ you see James or Felicity?
B No, I ^{9}_____ .
A ^{10}_____ Lara's parents there?
B No, they ^{11}_____ . I think they ^{12}_____ on holiday.
A And what time ^{13}_____ the party finish?
B At about 4 a.m.!

9C p74

6 Read this conversation at a ticket office. Write the words.

C A ^{1}r _e_ _t_ _u_ _r_ _n_ to Bath, please.
TS When do you want to ^{2}c _ _ _
   ^{3}b _ _ _ ?
C On Saturday.
TS OK. ^{4}T _ _ _ _ 's £38.90, please. Here's your ^{5}t _ _ _ _ _ _ .
C Thank you. What time's the ^{6}n _ _ _ train?
TS ^{7}T _ _ _ _ _ 's one at 3.15.
C Which ^{8}p _ _ _ _ _ _ _ m ?
TS ^{9}P _ _ _ _ _ _ m 2.
C What time does it ^{10}a _ _ _ _ _ ?
TS At 4.50.

9D p76

7 Write questions about the words in **bold** in sentences 1–8. Use these question words.

~~When~~	What	Who
Where	Why	How old
How much	How many	

1 I met John **two years ago**.
When did you meet John?
2 My favourite actor is **Brad Pitt**.
_____
3 We have **four** children.
_____
4 I was born **in Berlin**.
_____
5 My car is **11 years old**.
_____
6 My jacket was **£100**.
_____
7 I bought **a new dress**.
_____
8 I'm tired **because I started work at 5 a.m.**!
_____

Progress Portfolio 9

Tick (✓) the things you can do in English.

- [ ] I can talk about transport.
- [ ] I can talk about the past.
- [ ] I can understand a simple newspaper article.
- [ ] I can talk about things I do on holiday.
- [ ] I can ask and answer questions about the past.
- [ ] I can buy train tickets at a station.
- [ ] I can do a simple quiz.
- [ ] I can make questions with question words.

What do you need to study again? See Self-study DVD-ROM 9.

Extra Practice 10

10A p78

1 Cross out the wrong words.

1 **start** *a new job / a city / school*
2 **leave** *married / university / your job*
3 **do** *a course / a flat / an exam*
4 **move** *house / to Bath / a job*
5 **get** *engaged / school / married*
6 **look for** *a flat / engaged / a new job*

2 Fill in the gaps with the positive (+) or negative (–) form of *be going to* and these verbs.

~~watch~~	study	see
play	have	get up
stay	buy	move

1 (+) I*'m going to watch* a DVD when I get home.
2 (+) Megan _____ tennis next Saturday.
3 (+) I _____ in a hotel next weekend.
4 (–) They _____ house this year.
5 (+) We _____ English next year.
6 (–) Chris _____ early tomorrow.
7 (–) I _____ my brother this week.
8 (+) They _____ dinner in a French restaurant.
9 (–) We _____ a new car.

3 Choose the correct words in these time phrases.

1 *on /* (*in*) **2030**
2 *tomorrow / next* **month**
3 *in / at* **November**
4 *next / tomorrow* **evening**
5 *in / next* **week**
6 *tomorrow / in* **afternoon**
7 *on / in* **Monday**
8 *at / on* **March 30th**
9 *in / tomorrow* **night**
10 *in / next* **year**
11 *tomorrow / next* **day**
12 *in / next* **2020**

10B p80

4 Write the phrases with *have*, *watch*, *go* or *go to*.

1 g o s h o p p i n g
2 g _ to the g _ _
3 w _ _ _ _ _ the n _ _ _
4 g _ s _ _ _ _ _ _ _
5 h _ _ _ d _ _ _ _ _ with f _ _ _ _ _ _
6 g _ r _ _ _ _ _ _
7 h _ _ _ _ a p _ _ _ _
8 g _ to a p _ _ _
9 w _ _ _ _ s _ _ _ _ on T _

5 Write questions with *be going to*.

1 What / you / do this evening?
What are you going to do this evening?
2 When / they / move house?
_____
3 Who / he / stay with?
_____
4 Why / you / leave your job?
_____
5 Where / she / go on holiday?
_____

6 Fill in the gaps and write the short answers.

1 A *Are* you going to call her?
  B ✓ Yes, _____ .
2 A ___ Maria going to rent a car?
  B ✗ No, _____ .

3 A ___ they going to buy the flat?
  B ✓ _____ .
4 A ___ he going to leave his job?
  B ✗ _____ .
5 A ___ I going to see you again?
  B ✓ _____ .

10C p82

7 Find eight adjectives for feelings. (→↓)

H	A	P	P	Y	J	O	S
B	Q	A	N	G	R	Y	A
O	E	X	C	I	T	E	D
R	I	K	G	V	I	S	F
E	H	U	N	G	R	Y	M
D	E	A	J	L	E	N	B
S	C	A	R	E	D	U	C

8 Fill in the gaps with these words.

~~Have~~	See	in	you	with
good	much	lot	luck	

A ¹ *Have* a ² _____ holiday.
B Thanks a ³ _____ .
A ⁴ _____ you ⁵ _____ two weeks.
B Yes, see ⁶ _____ . And good ⁷ _____ ⁸ _____ your new job.
A Thanks very ⁹ _____ . Bye!

Progress Portfolio

Tick (✓) the things you can do in English.

- [ ] I can talk about future plans.
- [ ] I can use future time phrases.
- [ ] I can understand a simple conversation about the future.
- [ ] I can ask other people about their future plans.
- [ ] I can say how I feel.
- [ ] I can say goodbye and good luck.

What do you need to study again? See Self-study DVD-ROM 10.

Audio and Video Scripts

A

SUE Hello, my name's Sue. What's your name?
MARIO Hello, I'm Mario.
S Nice to meet you.
M You too.

B

ADAM Hi, Meg.
MEG Hi, Adam. How are you?
A I'm fine, thanks. And you?
M I'm OK, thanks.

A

A What's your home number?
B It's 020 7599 6320.
A 020 7599 6320.
B Yes, that's right.

B

A What's your mobile number?
B It's 07655 421769.
A 07655 421769.
B Yes, that's right.
A Thanks.

C

A What's your phone number in Madrid?
B It's 0034 91 532 67 53.
A 0034 91 …
B … 532 67 53.
A OK. Thank you.

EMEL Where are you from, Stefan?
STEFAN I'm from Russia. And you?
E I'm from Turkey.

Where are you from? | I'm from Russia. | And you? | I'm from Turkey.

ANSWERS 2a 3d 4c

A His name's Marcel and he's from France.
B Her name's Ayumi and she's from Japan.
C His name's Leon and he's from Poland.
D Her name's Mai and she's from Thailand.
E His name's Ricardo and he's from Colombia.
F Her name's Gita and she's from India.

1 u v 2 y i 3 g j 4 b v 5 a r 6 e i 7 b p 8 t d 9 u q 10 v w

SALLY Hello. What's your first name, please?
PABLO It's Pablo.
S What's your surname?
P Ortega.

S How do you spell that?
P O-r-t-e-g-a.
S Thank you, Pablo. Welcome to the class.
P Thank you.

1

SALLY Hello. What's your first name, please?
DOROTA It's Dorota.
S How do you spell that?
D D-o-r-o-t-a.
S Thanks. What's your surname?
D It's Kowalska.
S And how do you spell that?
D K-o-w-a-l-s-k-a.
S K-o-w-a-l-s-k-a. Thank you, Dorota. Welcome to the class.
D Thank you.

2

SALLY Hello. What's your first name, please?
KHALID It's Khalid.
S How do you spell that?
K K-h-a-l-i-d.
S Thanks. And what's your surname?
K Nazeer.
S OK. And how do you spell that, please?
K N-a-z-double e-r.
S N-a-z-double e-r. Thank you, Khalid. Welcome to the class.
K Thank you.

first name → What's your first name, please?
surname → What's your surname?
spell that → How do you spell that?

1

DOROTA Excuse me.
SALLY Yes, Dorota?
D What does answer mean?
S I ask a question, you say the answer.
D I'm sorry, I don't understand.
S OK. Question – What's your first name? Answer – It's Dorota.
D Ah, OK. I understand now. Thank you.

2

PABLO Excuse me.
SALLY Yes, Pablo?
P What's this in English?
S It's a pencil.
P Can you repeat that, please?
S Pencil.
P Pencil.
S Good.

3

SALLY What's the answer to question 1? Pablo?
PABLO I'm sorry, I don't know.
S Dorota?
DOROTA It's Brazil.
S That's right. Good.

KHALID Excuse me. How do you spell Brazil?
S B-r-a-z-i-l.
K OK. Thank you.

LINDA My name's Linda and I'm from London. I'm an English teacher at a language school near here. What's in my bag? Well, there are two books and an English dictionary. And here's my notebook, er, a pen – no, three pens – and my mobile.

BILL Hi, I'm Bill and I'm from Miami, in the USA. I'm in London for two days for work. What's in my bag? Well, my mobile, of course, and photos of my family – and, er, a pen. And, er, what else? Well, here's my lunch – an apple and a sandwich – no, two sandwiches!

CAROLINE Hello. My name's Caroline and I'm from Sydney, in Australia. I'm in the UK on holiday. In my bag there's, um, let's see, … my camera, two books about London, a notebook … um, oh yes, a pencil. Oh, and an umbrella, of course! Well, I am in England!

ANSWERS **A** British **B** German **C** Brazilian **D** American

I'm → I'm British.
You're → You're a student.
He's → He's German.
She's → She's Brazilian.
It's → It's American.

I'm not → I'm not American.
You aren't → You aren't a teacher.
He isn't → He isn't from Berlin.
She isn't → She isn't Australian.
It isn't → It isn't a Mercedes.

TINA Matt, do you want to see some photos of my friends?
MATT Sure.
T OK. This is a friend from Australia.
M What's his name?
T Gary. He's a doctor in Sydney.
M Oh, OK.
T And this is my friend Marco. He's a musician. He's very good.
M Is he Spanish?
T No, he isn't. He's from Mexico.
M Oh, right.
T And this is my friend Emma.
M That's a nice photo. Where's she from?
T She's from France. But she's a teacher in London now.

M Really? Hmm. She's very beautiful.
T Yes, she is – and she's married.
M Oh, right.
T And this is my friend Sofia. She's from Italy.
M Is she a musician?
T No, she isn't. She's an actress.
M Oh, OK. Is she married?
T Um, no, she's single.
M Really? What's her phone number?
T Matt!

CD1 ▶ 38

Mr → Mr Brown | Mrs → Mrs King | Ms → Ms King | Ms → Ms Roberts | Miss → Miss Roberts

CD1 ▶ 39

A
RECEPTIONIST Good morning, Mr Brown.
MR BROWN Good morning, Amanda.

B
MR BROWN Good afternoon, Mrs King.
MRS KING Good afternoon.

C
WAITER Good evening, sir.
MR BROWN Good evening.

D
MR BROWN Thank you very much. Good night.
WAITER Good night, sir.

CD1 ▶ 41

dot co dot u k → at city gym dot co dot u k → peter dot west at city gym dot co dot u k
dot com → at gmail dot com → frank robson one two three at gmail dot com
dot net → at webmail dot net → kim price nine at webmail dot net
dot org → at email dot org → rebecca dot taylor at email dot org

VIDEO ▶2 CD1 ▶ 42

PETER Well, that's our gym. What do you think?
KAREN Yes, it's very nice. So, how do I join?
P Well, first I need some personal information.
K Of course.
P OK. What's your first name, please?
K It's Karen.
P And what's your surname?
K It's Wendell.
P OK, um, how do you spell that, please?
K It's W-e-n-d-e-double l.
P Thank you. And what's your nationality?
K I'm British.
P OK. And what's your address?
K It's 7 Hatherley Road, Liverpool, L11 7HR.
P How do you spell Hatherley?
K H-a-t-h-e-r-l-e-y.
P So that's 7 Hatherley Road, Liverpool, L11 7HR.
K Yes, that's right.
P Ok, thanks. Right, er, next question. What's your mobile number?

K It's 07854 864247.
P 07854 … um …
K 864247.
P Thanks. And what's your email address?
K It's k.wendell9@gmail.com.
P So that's k.wendell9@gmail.com.
K Yes, that's right.
P OK, thanks a lot. Right, now let's talk about what type of membership is right for you.

CD1 ▶ 43

What's your first name, please?
What's your surname?
What's your nationality?
What's your address?
What's your mobile number?
What's your email address?

CD1 ▶ 48

1
WOMAN 1 Good morning, Tony.
TONY Good morning, Mrs Blake.
W1 Oh, is this your cat?
T Yes, his name's Charlie.
W1 How old is he?
T He's thirteen.

2
MAN 1 How old is your house, Tony?
TONY It's a hundred years old, I think.
M1 Oh, right.

3
TONY And this is Emily.
WOMAN 2 Hello, Emily.
EMILY Hello.
W2 How old are you?
E I'm nine.

4
MAN 2 Is that your car?
TONY Yes, it is.
M2 How old is it?
T It's twenty-one years old.
M2 Wow!

5
TONY Bonnie … come here … good girl.
WOMAN 3 What a nice dog. How old is she?
T She's seven. Or forty-nine, in dog years!

CD1 ▶ 49

ANSWERS 2 is 3 old 4 are 5 I'm

CD1 ▶ 55

1 We aren't from Italy, we're from Spain.
2 It's a new hotel, but it isn't very nice.
3 He's a doctor and he isn't married.
4 You aren't Australian, you're American.
5 I'm a manager and she's a musician.
6 They're actors, but they aren't very good.

CD1 ▶ 59

1 Nick is Fiona's husband.
2 Kevin is Nick's son.
3 Fiona is Kevin's mother.
4 Anne is Fiona's daughter.
5 Nick is Anne's father.

6 Anne is Kevin's sister.
7 Nick and Fiona are Kevin and Anne's parents.

CD1 ▶ 61

MARY I'm Mary and this is Sid, my husband. I'm 65 and Sid is 64 – like the Beatles song! This is a photo of our daughter Fiona and her family. Fiona's a teacher at a big school in Manchester. She's 43 now, or is it 44? No, she's 43. Her husband's name is Nick and he's a doctor. And I think he's a very good father.
And these are their two children – our grandchildren. This is Anne, our granddaughter. She's 14 and she's a very good musician. And this is our grandson, Kevin. He's 11 – oh no, he's 12 now. It's a very nice photo, I think.

CD1 ▶ 62

ANSWERS 2b 3e 4c 5a 6d

CD1 ▶ 63

a seventeen pounds b seventy p c a hundred dollars d twenty-one euros e thirty-five cents f twenty-one dollars fifty g three euros seventy-five h seven pounds sixty

CD1 ▶ 64

1
A Excuse me. How much is this watch?
B It's twenty-five pounds.

2
A This is very nice. How much is it?
B It's sixty-four dollars.

3
A How much are the pens?
B They're seventy p.
A OK. Two, please.

4
A These bags are beautiful. How much are they?
B They're forty-eight pounds fifty.
A OK, thank you.

5
A They're nice.
B Yes, but they're very expensive.
A How much are they?
B They're ninety-five euros.
A Oh …

CD1 ▶ 66

a coffee | a cappuccino | an espresso | a tea | a mineral water | an orange juice | a croissant | an egg sandwich | a cheese and tomato sandwich | a tuna salad

VIDEO ▶3 CD1 ▶ 67

ASSISTANT Hello. Can I help you?
CUSTOMER 1 Er, yes. An orange juice and a cheese and tomato sandwich, please.
A Sure. Anything else?
C1 No, that's all, thanks.
A Eat in or take away?

C1 Take away, please.
A OK, that's four pounds fifty-five, please.
C1 Here you are.
A OK. Enjoy your meal.
C1 Thanks a lot.
A You're welcome. Bye.
C1 Bye.

ASSISTANT Hi. Can I help you?
CUSTOMER 2 Yes, two cappuccinos, please.
A Sure. Anything else?
C2 Yes. A croissant and an egg sandwich, please.
A OK. Eat in or take away?
C2 Eat in, please.
A OK, that's eight pounds sixty, please.
C2 Here you are.
A Thank you. OK, here's your food. I'll bring the cappuccinos to your table.
C2 Thank you very much.
A You're welcome. Right, two cappuccinos …

CD1 ▶ 68

Can I help you?
Yes, two cappuccinos, please.
Sure. Anything else?
Yes, a croissant and an egg sandwich, please.
No, that's all, thanks.
Eat in or take away?
Eat in, please.
Take away, please.
OK, that's eight pounds sixty, please.
Thank you very much.
Thanks a lot.
You're welcome.

CD1 ▶ 71

FIONA What food and drink does my family like? Well, my husband Nick and I like a lot of the same things. We love coffee, but we like it black, not white. And we drink a lot of tea – it's very good for you, they say. And food, well, we don't eat meat, but we eat a lot of fish.
Our children, Anne and Kevin, well, they like eggs and they eat a lot of pasta. And they're children, so they love chocolate, of course!

CD2 ▶ 4

2 live 3 have 4 don't live 5 live 6 work 7 like 8 don't like 9 study 10 like

CD2 ▶ 8

1 Do you go to the cinema?
2 What food do you like?
3 Where do you go shopping?
4 Do you play video games?

CD2 ▶ 9

Where do you live?
What music do you like?
Do you go to concerts?
Do you like Mexican food?
Do you go to the cinema?
What food do you like?

Where do you go shopping?
Do you play video games?
Yes, I do.
No, I don't.

CD2 ▶ 11

this ➝ this map ➝ How much is this map?
these ➝ these birthday cards ➝ How much are these birthday cards?
that ➝ that big box of chocolates ➝ How much is that big box of chocolates?
those ➝ those batteries ➝ How much are those batteries?

VIDEO ▶ 4   CD2 ▶ 12

ANSWERS   1 £5.75 2 £2.99 3 £9.34
4 £1.79 5 £8.75 6 £12.33

CD2 ▶ 13

Excuse me. Do you have any maps of London?
Yes, they're over there.
How much is this map?
It's £5.75.
How much are these birthday cards?
They're £1.79 each.
Can I have that box of chocolates and these cards, please?
Sure. Anything else?
Yes, these sweets, please.
No, that's all, thanks.
OK, that's £12.33.
Here you are.
Thanks a lot.
Thanks very much.

CD2 ▶ 15

a second | a minute | an hour | a day | a week | a month | a year

CD2 ▶ 17

1
WOMAN Excuse me.
MAN Yes?
W What time is it, please?
M It's twenty to three.
W Thank you.

2
STUDENT Federico?
FEDERICO Yes?
S What time is your English class?
F It's at half past eight.

3
ANNOUNCER And the time is now six o'clock. Here is today's news, read by Graham Robertson.

4
SOPHIE Goodbye, Colin.
COLIN Bye, Sophie. See you at quarter to twelve tomorrow.
S Yes, see you.

5
TEACHER OK, that's it. Thanks a lot. See you on Wednesday at two thirty.
STUDENTS OK. / See you. / Bye. / Cheers.

CD2 ▶ 19

ANSWERS   b Friday and Saturday c 32
d morning e afternoon f Friday 13th
g Tuesday 13th h 7 hours i 11½ hours
j Sundays k Tuesdays l Thursdays

CD2 ▶ 24

ANSWERS   b 7.45 c 8.15 d 9.00 e 12.45
f 5.30 g 6.15 h 7.30

CD2 ▶ 26

like, likes | play, plays | start, starts | finish, finishes | have, has | study, studies | love, loves | go, goes | eat, eats | watch, watches | drink, drinks | read, reads

CD2 ▶ 27

ANSWERS   2 doesn't work 3 gets up
4 doesn't have 5 has 6 goes 7 leaves
8 starts 9 finishes 10 doesn't eat 11 has
12 gets 13 watches 14 don't work 15 have
16 talk

CD2 ▶ 29

TOM Here you are, Carol. A cheese sandwich and a cappuccino.
CAROL Thanks a lot, Tom. Oh look, there's Nadine!
T Who's Nadine?
C She works in the mobile phone shop with me. Nadine! Hi!
NADINE Hello, Carol! How are you?
C I'm fine, thanks. Nadine, this is my brother, Tom.
N Nice to meet you, Tom.
T You too. So, um, you work in the mobile phone shop with Carol.
N Yes, that's right. But I don't work in the week, only at the weekend.
T What do you do in the week?
N I'm a student at the university. I study English and Italian.
T Oh, OK. Where are you from?
N I'm from Germany. From Frankfurt.
T And where do you live in Manchester?
N I live near the university with two other students.
C Do you like Manchester?
N Yes, I do. The people are nice and there are a lot of things to do here.
T What do you do in your free time?
N I play tennis and, er, I go to the cinema a lot. And what about you, Tom? Are you a student?
T No, I'm a waiter. I work in a restaurant …

CD2 ▶ 32

chicken salad | vegetable lasagne | burger and chips | mushroom pizza | apple pie and cream | fruit salad | chocolate ice cream | strawberry ice cream | vanilla ice cream | a bottle of mineral water | still | sparkling | an orange juice | a coffee | a tea

MARTIN I don't know what to have.
LOUISE The lasagne looks nice.
M Yes, maybe.
WAITER Good evening. Are you ready to order?
L Yes. Can I have the chicken salad, please?
M And can I have the mushroom pizza?
W Certainly. What would you like to drink?
L An orange juice for me, please.
M And can we have a bottle of mineral water?
W Still or sparkling?
M Sparkling, please.
W OK. Thanks very much.

L That was very nice, thank you.
M Yes, the pizza was very good.
W Thank you very much. Would you like a dessert?
L Not for me, thanks.
M The apple pie for me, please.
L And two coffees, please.
W Of course.

M Excuse me. Can we have the bill, please?
W Of course.
M Thanks a lot. (to Louise) Would you like to go to Cambridge?
L This weekend? Yes, that's a good idea.
M OK. A weekend in Cambridge. Fantastic! (to waiter) Thank you.

always | usually | sometimes |
not usually | never |
every day | every week | every month |
every year |
every morning | every afternoon |
every evening | every night |
every Sunday | every Friday evening |
every six weeks | every four years

BRUCE What do you usually do on Sundays, Amy?
AMY Well, I usually do the same things every Sunday. I always get up at about seven o'clock.
B That's very early for a Sunday!
A Yes, but I like mornings. I always have breakfast with my husband, Lucas.
B Do you always have the same breakfast?
A Yes, we do. We have eggs, orange juice and lots of coffee.
B That sounds good.
A Yes, it is. And after breakfast my sister, Becky, usually phones me from England. It's afternoon there, of course.
B Right.
A We usually talk for about half an hour, then I do my Spanish homework.
B Really? You study Spanish?
A Yes, I go to a class every Thursday evening.
B Oh, right. Is your Spanish good?

A Well, it's not bad. And we usually go to Lucas's parents for lunch.
B Oh, nice.
A And we watch a DVD every Sunday evening. It's a great way to finish the weekend.
B Well, I think you have a very nice Sunday routine.
A Yes, I love Sundays. And what about you? What's your Sunday routine?

Listening Test (see Teacher's Book)

ANSWERS 2 are 3 's 4 are 5 's 6 are 7 's 8 are

SUSAN Well, here we are, Isabel. Come in. Welcome to my home.
ISABEL Thanks, Susan. Oh, what a beautiful flat!
S Thanks a lot.
I Do you like living here?
S Yes, I do. It's a nice road and the people are very friendly.
I That's good. Are there any shops near here?
S Yes, there are. In this road there's, um, a small supermarket, a chemist's and a post office.
I Is there a bank?
S No, there isn't. But there's a cashpoint at the post office. And there are a lot of banks in the centre of Bath, of course.
I OK. Are we near the city centre?
S Yes, it's only two miles from here.
I Oh, right. And can I get to the centre by train?
S No, there isn't a station near here, but, um, there are buses to the city centre every ten minutes. The bus stop's near the post office.
I That's good to know. And what about places to eat?
S Well, there aren't any good restaurants near here, but, um, there are some very nice restaurants in the centre.
I Great! Maybe we can go out for dinner this evening.
S Yes, that's a good idea. Right, this is your room …

There's an expensive market.
There are some old buildings.
There isn't an airport.
There aren't any museums.
Is there a post office?
Yes, there is.
No, there isn't.
Are there any nice old cafés?
Yes, there are.
No, there aren't.

MARTIN Good morning.
ASSISTANT Hello. Can I help you?
M Yes, please. Do you have a map of Cambridge city centre?
A Yes, of course. Here you are.
M Thanks a lot.
LOUISE And when is Kettle's Yard art gallery open?
A It's open from 11.30 a.m. to 5 p.m.
L Is it open every day?
A No, it's closed on Mondays.
L OK. Thanks.
A Can I help you with anything else?
M Er, yes, please. Where's the Fitzwilliam Museum?
A It's in Trumpington Street.
M Can you show me on this map?
A Yes, of course. Here it is. It's about five minutes away.
M Thank you.
L Er, one more thing, if that's OK. We want to see the university. Can we book a walking tour here?
A Yes, of course. They start at 11 a.m. and 1 p.m. every day.
L How much are they?
A They're £17.50 per person.
L OK, thanks a lot. We'll think about it.
A No problem. Have a nice day.
L You too.
M Bye.
A Goodbye.

2 When 3 from 4 to 5 Is it 6 on 7 where's 8 in 9 map 10 Here it is. 11 afternoon 12 of 13 here you are 14 book 15 at 16 day 17 are 18 person

LISA My favourite colour is pink and this is my favourite dress. I love this coat too, and these shoes. I have about … about thirty pairs of shoes at home, but I never wear trainers. I don't think they look good on girls.
BRAD I usually wear jeans, a T-shirt and, um, these trainers. My clothes are usually blue or black, and I never wear brown. Oh, and this is my favourite jacket, this black one. It's about five years old and I love it!
WAYNE I love shopping for clothes and I have about ten suits at home. I always wear a suit and tie for work, and, er, this is my favourite shirt, this blue one. But I never wear jeans. They don't look good on me.
MONICA I usually wear a skirt for work, like today, and I love wearing jumpers when it's cold. And these are my favourite boots. I wear them all the time. But, um, but I never wear dresses. I don't like them.

My favourite colour is pink.
This is my favourite jacket.
These are my favourite boots.
What's your favourite colour?
Who's your favourite actor?

CD2 63

ANSWERS 2 her 3 it 4 him 5 them 6 me

CD2 66

1 I can play the guitar.
2 You can't cook.
3 He can play basketball.
4 She can't drive.
5 We can't speak French.
6 They can sing very well.

CD2 67

MRS TAYLOR Hello, Natalia. My name's
    Gillian Taylor. Nice to meet you.
NATALIA You too.
MRS T Right, we want an au pair to help us
    with our two children, Megan and Harry.
N OK. How old are they?
MRS T Megan's twelve and Harry's ten.
N Right.
MRS T So, er, I have some questions if that's
    OK.
N Yes, of course.
MRS T Great. OK. Can you cook?
N Yes, I can. I love cooking and I often cook
    dinner for my family at home.
MRS T That's good. Can you drive?
N Yes, I can.
MRS T OK, great. And can you speak
    French or German? The children both
    study French at school and Megan starts
    German next year.
N Um, I can't speak German, but I can
    speak French.
MRS T Oh, that's good. And what about free
    time activities? Can you swim?
N Yes, I can. I love swimming.
MRS T And can you play tennis?
N No, I can't. But I can play football.
MRS T Oh, that's good. The children both
    love playing football. And what about
    music? Can you play the piano?
N No, I can't. But I can sing and I can play
    the guitar.
MRS T Oh, right. Megan plays the guitar
    too. Maybe you can help her.
N Yes, of course.
MRS T OK, one last question.
N Yes, Mrs Taylor?
MRS T When can you start?

VIDEO 7 **CD3** 2

ANSWERS 1 museum 2 museum
3 on 4 next to 5 café 6 on 7 next to
8 post office 9 near 10 can 11 bank
12 in 13 bank 14 left

CD3 3

Excuse me. Where's the museum?
Excuse me. Is there a bank near here?
Go along this road and turn left.
Go along this road and turn right.
That's Park Street.
The museum is on the right, next to the
theatre.
The bank is on the left, opposite the station.
It's over there, near the cinema.

CD3 4

ANSWERS 1 me 2 here 3 right 4 on 5 near
6 Where's 7 over 8 next to 9 near 10 along
11 right 12 hotel

CD3 6

INTERVIEWER Excuse me?
SAM Yes?
I Can I ask you some questions about how
    you use the internet?
S Yes, sure.
I Great, thanks a lot. OK. First question.
    Do you watch TV programmes online?
S Well, I watch videos online, but not TV
    programmes. I love YouTube. It's my
    favourite website.
I OK, thanks. And what about the radio?
    Do you listen to the radio online?
S Er, no, I don't. I never listen to the radio.
I OK. And are you on Facebook?
S Yes, I am. I'm on Twitter too, but I don't
    use it very much.
I Right. Do you chat to friends and family
    online?
S Yes, sometimes. My sister lives in Poland
    and we chat online every week.
I OK. Do you buy and sell things online?
S Yes, I do. I buy DVDs on Amazon and
    then sell them again on eBay.
I And do you use the internet to book
    flights or holidays?
S No, I don't. My wife always does that.
I OK. Two more questions. Do you read
    people's blogs?
S Er, no, I don't. Sorry. I don't like blogs
    very much.
I And the last question. Do you download
    music?
S Yes, I do, and then I listen to it on my
    phone when I'm on the train.
I OK, thanks a lot, that's great.
S No problem. Bye.

CD3 12

I was at the World Cup Final.
We were near the Opera House.
The stadium wasn't full.
They weren't very happy.
I was very young at the time.
It was a great match!
It was a fantastic New Year!
There were some amazing fireworks!
The concert wasn't very long.

CD3 15

FRIEND Sunil, are you busy on Sunday?
SUNIL Yes, I am, sorry. It's my wedding
    anniversary on Sunday.
F Oh, happy anniversary!
S Thanks a lot. It's amazing that my
    wedding was five years ago.
F Was it here in the UK?
S No, it wasn't. It was in Mumbai, in India.
F Really?
S Yes. Pria was born in London, but her
    father's parents live in Mumbai.
F Right. And how old were you and Pria on
    your wedding day?
S I was 28 and Pria was 24.
F Oh. Was it a big wedding?
S Yes, it was. There were two hundred and
    fifty people there.
F Oh, wow! Were all your family at the
    wedding?
S No, they weren't. My sister was in the
    USA, so she wasn't there. But my parents
    and my two brothers were there.
F And was there a party after the wedding?
S Yes, there was – for three days!
F Three days?! That's amazing!
S Yes, there was fantastic Indian food and a
    lot of dancing. I was very tired at the end!
F I'm sure you were. So what are your plans
    for Saturday?

CD3 16

Where was the wedding?
How old were Sunil and Pria?
How many people were at the wedding?
Where was Sunil's sister?
Was she at the wedding?
Yes, she was.
No, she wasn't.
Were they at the wedding?
Yes, they were.
No, they weren't.
Where was Pria born?
She was born in London.
When were you born?
I was born in nineteen ninety-one.

CD3 21

1
A What's the date today?
B It's June 22nd.
A Thanks a lot.
2
A When's your birthday?
B March 30th.
A Really? That's my birthday too!
3
A When's your wedding anniversary?
B It's on October 3rd.
A Oh, that's next week!
4
A When do you start your new job?
B On April 1st.
A Really? Er … good luck!

DANNY Here's your croissant. The cappuccinos are on their way.

KAREN Thanks a lot.

D No problem. What time's your driving test?

K Eleven thirty. But I have a driving lesson at half past ten.

D Oh, OK. What's this?

K It's a present. Happy birthday for yesterday!

D Really? Thanks, Karen. Wow, what a great shirt! Thanks a lot.

K I'm pleased you like it.

ASSISTANT Here are your cappuccinos.

D Thank you very much.

K So, what shall we do this evening? We need to celebrate your birthday.

D I don't know. What do you think?

K Why don't we go out for dinner? We can go to that nice Mexican restaurant near your flat.

D No, I don't think so. I go there every week.

K OK, well, let's go to a club.

D Maybe. But they're always very busy on Fridays.

K Hmm.

D I know! Why don't we go to the cinema?

K Yes, that's a good idea. Do you know what's on?

D Well, there's that new Johnny Depp film. People say it's very good.

K Great! Where shall we meet?

D Let's meet at the cinema.

K OK. What time shall we meet?

D About seven thirty. Then we can have a drink first.

K Yes, good idea. So, tell me about your birthday. What was your best present?

D Well, this shirt, of course!

CD3 23

What shall we do this evening?
Let's go to a club.
Why don't we go to the cinema?
Yes, that's a good idea.
Maybe.
No, I don't think so.
Where shall we meet?
Let's meet at the cinema.
What time shall we meet?
About seven thirty.

CD3 24

GEORGE What shall we do tomorrow evening, Jessica?

JESSICA Why don't we go to the cinema?

G No, I don't think so.

J OK. Let's go to that Indian restaurant in Old Street.

G Yes, that's a good idea. Where shall we meet?

J Let's meet at the restaurant.

G OK. What time shall we meet?

J About quarter to eight.

G Great! See you there!

CD3 26

a 365 b 999 c 17,000 d 62,400 e 250,000
f 1,200,000 g 18,000,000

CD3 27

ANSWERS a 30,000 b 125,000 c 150,000
d 1,500 e 177,500 f 5 million g 70 million

CD3 28

OWEN Do you like going to festivals, Ella?

ELLA Yes, I do. I go to about four festivals every year.

O Really? What's your favourite?

E Er, probably Glastonbury, I think.

O Oh, why's that?

E Well, I like it because there are lots of different things you can do. There are lots of famous bands on every day, of course. But when you don't want to listen to music, you can go to the theatre, watch a film or go shopping in the market.

O That sounds interesting.

E Yes, and the best thing about the festival is all the nice people you meet. I love sitting in cafés and talking to people I don't know – and I always make a lot of new friends. And what about you? Do you go to festivals?

O Well, my brother and I went to the Rio Carnival in February.

E Really? Wow! How was it?

O It was amazing! There were thousands of people in the street every night, and everyone was dancing and having a fantastic time. And I love Brazilian music.

E Yes, me too.

O But the hotel was expensive, and it was sometimes difficult to sleep because of the noise.

E Yes, of course. And can you dance the samba like a Brazilian?

O Er, no, I can't. My dancing is terrible! But I have a lot of new friends from the festival that I can chat to on Facebook!

CD3 34

visit, visited | watch, watched | play, played | hate, hated | walk, walked | work, worked | live, lived | want, wanted | love, loved | talk, talked | start, started | finish, finished

CD3 35

bought | came | got | gave | went | had | left | met | told | wrote

CD3 37

1 I liked your photos. I like your photos.
2 We live in Spain. We lived in Spain.
3 They arrived at ten. They arrive at ten.
4 We talk every day. We talked every day.
5 I want to go home. I wanted to go home.
6 They played football a lot. They play football a lot.

SALLY A return to London, please.

TICKET SELLER When do you want to come back?

S Tomorrow evening.

TS OK. That's £46.70, please. Here are your tickets.

S Thanks. What time's the next train?

TS There's one at 10.23.

S OK. Which platform?

TS Platform three.

S Right. And what time does it arrive in London?

TS At 11.56.

S Thanks a lot. Bye. [on phone] Oh, hi there. Yes, I just got my ticket. I get to London at about midday. So, where shall we meet?

CD3 45

ANSWERS 2 That's 3 your 4 next 5 at
6 Which 7 does 8 At 9 a lot

SALLY Hi, Rob. How are you?

ROB I'm fine, thanks. Did you have a good weekend?

S Yes, I did, thanks.

R What did you do?

S I went away for the weekend.

R Oh, nice! Where did you go?

S I went to London to see my brother, Chris.

R Did you have a good time?

S Yes, I love going to London. It's an amazing city.

R So, what did you do there?

S Well, on Saturday afternoon we went shopping in Oxford Street. It was very busy, of course, but I love shopping there. And in the evening we went to the theatre in the West End.

R Oh, really? What did you see?

S *Les Misérables*. You know, the musical.

R Oh, right. Did you enjoy it?

S Yes, it was fantastic! We had a great evening. And on Sunday morning we went to the National Gallery. Chris doesn't like art galleries very much, but I love them. Then we had lunch in a café in Leicester Square with some friends from university.

R That sounds nice.

S Yes, it was. And what about you? What did you do at the weekend?

R Well, on Saturday evening we went to that new Turkish restaurant on Station Road.

S Oh yes, I know it. Did you have a good time?

R Yes, the waiters were very friendly and the food was fantastic!

S Oh, it's time to go – we're late for class!

R Oh, yes! See you later.

Did you have a good weekend?
What did you do at the weekend?
Where did you go?
What did you do there?
Did you have a good time?
What did you see?
Did you enjoy it?

JACKIE Mark, do you want to do a quiz?
MARK Yes, I love doing quizzes. What's the first question?
J OK. What is the capital of Australia? Is it Canberra, Sydney or Melbourne?
M That's an easy question. It's Sydney, of course.
J No, you're wrong. It's Canberra.
M Really? Oh.
J Here's the second question. Where were the two thousand and eight Olympic Games? Were they in London, Athens or Beijing?
M I think they were in London.
J No, you're wrong again, Mark! The London Olympics were in twenty twelve. The two thousand and eight Olympics were in Beijing.
M Oh yes, of course.
J Question three. How old is the Earth? Is it ten billion years old, four and a half billion years old or one and a half billion years old?
M Er, I think it's ten billion years old.
J No, it's four and a half billion years old. You aren't very good at this, are you Mark?
M Well, they're very difficult questions!
J OK, question four. Who was the director of the films *Jaws*, *E.T.* and *Jurassic Park*? Was it James Cameron, Martin Scorsese or Steven Spielberg?
M I think it was Steven Spielberg.
J Yes, you've got one right! Well done! OK, question five. When did the first man walk on the moon? Was it nineteen forty-nine, nineteen sixty-nine or nineteen eighty-nine?
M Was it nineteen sixty-nine?
J Yes, that's correct. But then, you probably watched it live on TV, didn't you?
M Hey, I'm not that old!
J Hmm. Right, question six. How much does the President of the USA earn a year? Is it four hundred thousand dollars, seven hundred thousand dollars, or a million dollars?
M I don't know, but I think it's seven hundred thousand dollars.
J No, it's four hundred thousand dollars.
M Really? Oh, I got that wrong then.
J Yes, you did. Question seven. How many countries are there in Africa? Are there fourteen, thirty-four or fifty-four?
M Er … thirty-four?

J No, you're wrong again! It's fifty-four! And the last question. Why is the English town of Stratford-upon-Avon famous? Is it because …
M That's easy. It's because William Shakespeare was born in Stratford.
J Correct.
M So, how many did I get right?
J Er, let's see …

do a computer course → I'm going to /tə/ do a computer course.
leave his job → He's going to /tə/ leave his job.
travel around the UK → We're going to /tə/ travel around the UK.
start university this year → I'm not going to /tə/ start university this year.
stay here for very long → She isn't going to /tə/ stay here for very long.
live in São Paulo → They aren't going to /tə/ live in São Paulo.

JASON Hello, Andy.
ANDY Hi, Jason. Hi, Rosie.
ROSIE Hi.
J Busy day?
A Yes, Mondays are always busy. You?
J Yes, we had a lot of new customers today. And it's going to be difficult without Rosie.
A What do you mean?
J Don't you know? Rosie's going to move to South Africa next month.
A South Africa?! Really?
R Yes, this is my last week at the bank.
A Wow! I didn't know that. Why South Africa?
R My husband, Freddie, is going to work for a travel company in Cape Town.
A OK. And what about you? What are you going to do?
R I don't know. I'm going to look for a job when I arrive.
J Are you going to sell your flat?
R No, we're not. My two brothers are going to live there.
A That's a good idea. Are you going to have a party before you leave?
R No, but Freddie and I are going to have dinner with some friends in a restaurant next Friday. You know, to say goodbye. Er, would you like to come, Andy?
A Oh, yes, please. Um, thanks very much.
R Great. Oh, and Jason's going to be there, of course.
A Oh really? Er, maybe I'm busy on Friday.
J Ha ha, very funny!
A Anyway, I'm going to go to the cinema this evening. Do you want to come?
J Maybe. What are you going to see?
A Well, it's called *Frank's Happiness*, and it's about a man who …

What are you going to do next weekend?
What are you going to do after class?
When are you going to do your homework?
What time are you going to get up tomorrow?
Where are you going to have dinner tomorrow evening?
Where are you going to go on holiday next year?

VIDEO ▶ 10

ANSWERS 2 journey 3 London 4 two 5 ten 6 this evening 7 day 8 driving test 9 course 10 September 11 job

Have a good journey.
Thanks a lot.
Have a good holiday.
Have a good day.
Have a good weekend.
Have a good birthday.
Have a good time.
See you in September.
Yes, see you.
See you in two hours.
See you this evening.
See you on Monday.
See you soon.
See you later.
Good luck with your new job.
Thanks very much.
Good luck with your driving test.
Good luck with your exam.
Good luck with your new school.
Good luck with your English test.

A
ALAN What are you going to do after work?
JANE I'm going to have dinner with friends.
A Oh, nice. Have a good time.
J Thanks a lot. And good luck with your exam.
A Thanks very much. See you tomorrow.
J Yes, see you. Bye!

B
RYAN I'm going to go on holiday next week.
LILY Really? Where are you going?
R To Edinburgh, in Scotland.
L Well, have a good holiday.
R Thanks. Oh, and good luck with your new job.
L Thanks a lot.

Listening Test (see Teacher's Book)

Language Summary 1

1.1 ▶ Numbers 0–12   1A **7** p7

0	zero	3	three	6	six	9	nine	11	eleven
1	one	4	four	7	seven	10	ten	12	twelve
2	two	5	five	8	eight				

1.2 ▶ Countries   1B **1** p8

1	the USA	4	the UK	7	Italy	10	Russia
2	Mexico	5	Germany	8	Turkey	11	China
3	Brazil	6	Spain	9	Egypt	12	Australia

1.3 ▶ The alphabet   1C **1** p10

Aa Bb Cc Dd Ee Ff Gg Hh Ii Jj Kk
Ll Mm Nn Oo Pp Qq Rr Ss Tt Uu
Vv Ww Xx Yy Zz

TIP • **pink** letters = vowels, **blue** letters = consonants

1.4 ▶ Things in your bag (1)   1C **6** p10

1 a bag
2 an apple
3 a dictionary
4 a book
5 a notebook
6 a mobile
7 a pen
8 a pencil
9 an umbrella

TIPS • We can say *a mobile*, *a phone* or *a mobile phone*.
• UK: *a mobile (phone)* = US: *a cell (phone)*

1.5 ▶ *a* and *an*   1C **8** p11

- We use **a** with nouns that begin with a **consonant** sound: *a **b**ag*, *a **d**ictionary*, *a **p**en*, etc.
- We use **an** with nouns that begin with a **vowel** sound: *an **a**pple*, *an **u**mbrella*, etc.

1.6 ▶ People 1D **1** p12

a baby   a man   a woman   a boy   a girl

1.7 ▶ Things
1D **2** p12

1 a chair
2 a watch
3 a computer
4 a diary
5 a sandwich
6 a table
7 a camera

1.8 ▶ Plurals   1D **4** p12

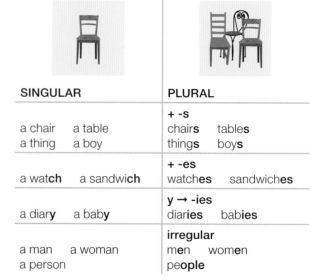

SINGULAR		PLURAL	
		+ -s	
a chair	a table	chairs	tables
a thing	a boy	things	boys
		+ -es	
a watch	a sandwich	watches	sandwiches
		y → -ies	
a diary	a baby	diaries	babies
		irregular	
a man	a woman	men	women
a person		people	

TIP • We also add *-es* to words ending in *-s*, *-ss*, *-sh*, *-x* and *-z*: *bus* → *bus**es***, *class* → *class**es***, etc.

1.1 ▶ *I, my, you, your* 1A 3 p6

I'm Stefan.   How are **you**?
I'm fine, thanks.   Nice to meet **you**.
My name's Emel.   What's **your** name?

TIPS • *I / you* + **verb** (*I* **read**, *you* **listen**, etc.)
• *my / your* + **noun** (*my* **name**, *your* **book**, etc.)
• *I'm = I am; name's = name is*

1.2 ▶ *he, his, she, her* 1B 7 p9

What's **his** name?   What's **her** name?
His name's Stefan.   **Her** name's Emel.
Where's **he** from?   Where's **she** from?
He's from Russia.   **She**'s from Turkey.

TIPS • *he / his* = 🧍   *she / her* = 🧍
• *he / she* + **verb**, *his / her* + **noun**

1.1 ▶ Saying hello 1A 1 2 p6

Hello, I'm Stefan. What's your name?

Hello, my name's Emel.

Nice to meet you.

You too.

Hi, Anita.

Hi, Tim. How are you?

I'm fine, thanks. And you?

I'm OK, thanks.

1.2 ▶ Introducing people 1A 6 p6

Polly, this is David.

Hello, David. Nice to meet you.

You too.

1.3 ▶ Phone numbers 1A 8 p7

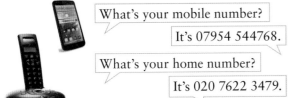

What's your mobile number?

It's 07954 544768.

What's your home number?

It's 020 7622 3479.

TIP • In phone numbers 0 = *oh* and 44 = *double four.*

1.4 ▶ Saying goodbye 1A 11 p7

Goodbye, Miki.

Bye, Lucy. See you soon.

Yes, see you.

1.5 ▶ *Where are you from?* 1B 5 p8

Where are you from, Stefan?

I'm from Russia. And you?

I'm from Turkey.

TIP • We can also say *I'm from* + city: *I'm from Moscow.*

1.6 ▶ First names and surnames 1C 3 p10

What's your first name, please?

It's Pablo.

What's your surname?

Ortega.

How do you spell that?

O-r-t-e-g-a.

1.7 ▶ Classroom language 1C 11 p11

Excuse me.

Can you repeat that, please?

What does (answer) mean?

I'm sorry, I don't know.

I'm sorry, I don't understand.

How do you spell (Brazil)?

What's this in English?

TIP • We can say *Can you repeat that, please?* or *Can you say that again, please?*

Look at Classroom Instructions p135.

Language Summary 2

VOCABULARY

2.1 ▶ Nationalities   2A 1 p14

countries	nationalities
I'm from Italy.	*I'm Italian.*
Italy	Italian
Brazil	Brazilian
Russia	Russian
the USA	American
Germany	German
Egypt	Egyptian
Australia	Australian
Mexico	Mexican
Turkey	Turkish
the UK	British
Spain	Spanish
China	Chinese
Japan	Japanese
France	French
Colombia	Colombian

2.2 ▶ Jobs   2B 1 p16

a sales assistant   a manager   a teacher

a taxi driver   a doctor   a musician

a police officer   an actor / an actress   a waiter / a waitress

TIPS • In the Language Summaries we only show the main stress (•) in words and phrases.

• We use **a** or **an** with jobs: *He's a doctor.*

2.3 ▶ Titles   2C 1 p18

Mr	a man (married or single)
Mrs / Ms	a married woman
Ms / Miss	a single woman

TIP • *Mr, Mrs, Ms* or *Miss* + surname: *Mr Brown, Mrs King, Ms Roberts*, etc.

2.4 ▶ Greetings   2C 2 p18

TIPS • *Good morning, Good afternoon* and *Good evening* = *Hello*
• *Good night* = *Goodbye*

2.5 ▶ Numbers 13–100   2D 1 2 5 p20

13 thirteen	21 twenty-one	30 thirty
14 fourteen	22 twenty-two	40 forty
15 fifteen	23 twenty-three	50 fifty
16 sixteen	24 twenty-four	60 sixty
17 seventeen	25 twenty-five	70 seventy
18 eighteen	26 twenty-six	80 eighty
19 nineteen	27 twenty-seven	90 ninety
20 twenty	28 twenty-eight	100 a hundred
	29 twenty-nine	

2.1 ▸ *be* (singular): positive   2A 4 p14

POSITIVE (+)

I'm (= I am)	I'm British.
you're (= you are)	You're a student.
he's (= he is)	He's German.
she's (= she is)	She's Brazilian.
it's (= it is)	It's American.

TIP • We use *it* for a thing (*a car*, *a book*, etc.):
It's a German car.
It's an English book.

2.2 ▸ *be* (singular): negative   2A 7 p15

NEGATIVE (–)

I'm not (= am not)	I'm not American.
you aren't (= are not)	You aren't a teacher.
he isn't (= is not)	He isn't from Berlin.
she isn't (= is not)	She isn't Australian.
it isn't (= is not)	It isn't a Mercedes.

TIPS • We can also say *you're not*, *he's not*, *she's not*
and *it's not*:
You're not a teacher.
He's not from Berlin.
She's not Australian.
It's not a Mercedes.
• We can't say ~~I amn't.~~

2.3 ▸ *be* (singular): *Wh-* questions
2B 3 p16

WH- QUESTIONS (?)

Where am I?
Where are you from?
Where's he / she / it from?
What's your name?
What's his / her name?
What's your job?
What's his / her job?

TIPS • *Where* asks about a place (*Turkey*, *London*, etc.).
• *What* asks about a thing (*a name*, *a job*, etc.).
• *Where's … ? = Where is … ?*
• *What's … ? = What is … ?*
• We can't write ~~Where'm I?~~ or ~~Where're you from?~~
• We also make questions with *How*: *How are you?*

2.4 ▸ *be* (singular): *yes / no* questions and short answers   2B 6 p17

YES / NO QUESTIONS (?)	SHORT ANSWERS
Am I in this class?	Yes, you **are**. / No, you **aren't**.
Are you from Russia?	Yes, I **am**. / No, I'm **not**.
Is he a doctor?	Yes, he **is**. / No, he **isn't**.
Is she Italian?	Yes, she **is**. / No, she **isn't**.
Is it Japanese?	Yes, it **is**. / No, it **isn't**.

TIPS • We can also say: *No, you're not. No, he's not.*
No, she's not. and *No, it's not.*
• We can't say ~~Yes, you're.~~, ~~Yes, I'm.~~, ~~Yes, he's.~~,
~~Yes, she's.~~ or ~~Yes, it's.~~

REAL WORLD ▸

2.1 ▸ Email addresses   2C 3 p18

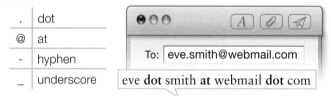

.	dot
@	at
-	hyphen
_	underscore

To: eve.smith@webmail.com

eve **dot** smith **at** webmail **dot** com

2.2 ▸ Personal information questions
2C 6 p19

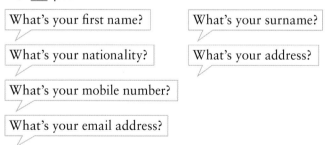

What's your first name?

What's your surname?

What's your nationality?

What's your address?

What's your mobile number?

What's your email address?

2.3 ▸ *How old … ?*   2D 8 p20

How old is your house?

It's a hundred years old.

How old are you?

I'm thirty.

TIPS • We don't usually say *years old* for people: *I'm thirty.,*
Emily's nine., etc.
• We say *I'm thirty.* not ~~I have thirty.~~ or ~~I'm thirty years.~~

Language Summary 3

 DVD-ROM 3

3.1 ▸ Adjectives (1)

3A **1** p22

friendly unfriendly

beautiful ugly

big small

good bad

hot cold

expensive cheap

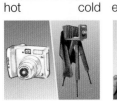
new old

nice

3.2 ▸ Word order with adjectives; *very* 3A **2** p22

- **Adjectives** go after **be**:
  Your watch is nice.
- **Adjectives** go before **nouns**:
  It's a new car.
- **Adjectives** are not plural with **plural nouns**:
  They're good friends.
  not *They're goods friends.*
- We put **very** before **adjectives**:
  It's very hot.

28°
It's hot.

42°
It's very hot.

TIP • Notice the word order in questions: **Are** you cold?, **Is** the camera expensive?, **Is** he friendly?, etc.

3.3 ▸ Family 3B **2** p24 **7** p25

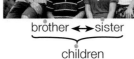
parents
husband ⟷ wife
father (dad)
mother (mum)
son
daughter
brother ⟷ sister
children

grandparents
grandfather grandmother
grandson granddaughter
grandchildren

TIPS • The plural of *wife* is *wives* not ~~wifes~~.
• The singular of *children* is *a child*.

TIP • The singular of *grandchildren* is *a grandchild*.

3.4 ▸ Food and drink (1) 3C **6** p26

a coffee

a cappuccino

an espresso

a tea

a mineral water

an orange juice

a croissant

an egg sandwich

a cheese and tomato sandwich

a tuna salad

TIP • We can say *a white coffee* (with milk) and *a black coffee* (no milk).

3.5 ▸ Food and drink (2) 3D **1** p28

1 fruit	9 fish
2 tea	10 rice
3 coffee	11 meat
4 vegetables	12 cheese
5 orange juice	13 eggs
6 milk	14 sugar
7 bread	15 pasta
8 water	16 chocolate

3.6 ▸ *love, like, eat, drink, a lot of* 3D **3** p28

I **love** chocolate.

I **like** fish.

I **eat a lot of** rice.

I **drink a lot of** coffee.

3.1 ▶ *be* (plural): positive and negative
3A 6 p23

POSITIVE (+)

we're (= we are)	We're in a small hotel.
you're (= you are)	You're from the UK.
they're (= they are)	They're very big.

NEGATIVE (–)

we aren't (= are not)	We aren't in the hotel now.
you aren't	You aren't from Turkey.
they aren't	They aren't very expensive.

TIPS • With plural nouns we write *people are* not *people're*, *rooms are* not *rooms're*, etc.

• *You* is singular and plural: *You're **a** student. You're student**s**.*

• We can also say *we're not*, *you're not* and *they're not*.

3.2 ▶ *be* (plural): questions and short answers
3A 11 p23

WH- QUESTIONS (?)

Where	are	we?
Where	are	you?
Where	are	they?
Where	are	Liz and Steve?

YES / NO QUESTIONS (?)	SHORT ANSWERS
Are we in room 216?	Yes, you are. No, you aren't.
Are you in London?	Yes, we are. No, we aren't.
Are they in a big hotel?	Yes, they are. No, they aren't.

TIP • We can also say: *No, we're not. No, you're not.* and *No, they're not.*

3.3 ▶ Possessive *'s*
3B 4 p24

• We use a name (*Nick*, etc.) or a noun for a person (*sister*, etc.) + *'s* for the possessive.
Fiona is Nick's wife. It's my sister's car.

TIPS • *'s* can mean *is* or the **possessive**: *Anne's my sister.* (*'s* = *is*); *Kevin is Nick's son.* (*'s* = possessive)

• We can also use *'s* with other nouns for people: *It's my **teacher's** car. It's his **friend's** camera.*, etc.

• For plural nouns, we write *s'*: *It's my parents' house. He's my friends' son.*

3.4 ▶ Subject pronouns (*I, you*, etc.) and possessive adjectives (*my, your*, etc.)
3B 9 p25

subject pronouns	I	you	he	she	it	we	they
possessive adjectives	my	your	his	her	its	our	their

• We use **subject pronouns** with verbs: *I'm, you listen, they read*, etc.

• We use **possessive adjectives** with nouns: *my sister, your family, their cat*, etc.
*I'm Mary and this is Sid, **my** husband.*
***Her** husband's name is Nick and **he**'s a doctor.*
*These are **their** two children – **our** grandchildren.*
***It**'s a very nice photo, I think.*

REAL WORLD

3.1 ▶ Money and prices
3C 1 p26

| ten pounds | ten p
(p = pence) | ten (pounds) fifty | ten euros | ten dollars | ten cents |

3.2 ▶ *How much ... ?*
3C 4 p26

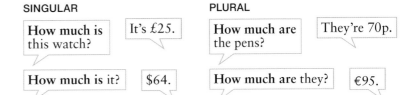

SINGULAR

How much is this watch? — It's £25.

How much is it? — $64.

PLURAL

How much are the pens? — They're 70p.

How much are they? — €95.

3.3 ▶ In a café
3C 9 p27

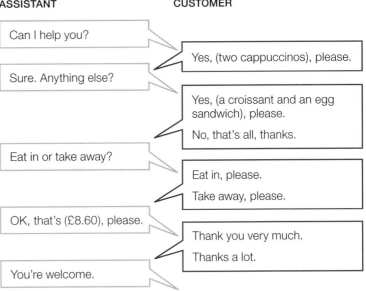

ASSISTANT / CUSTOMER

Can I help you? — Yes, (two cappuccinos), please.

Sure. Anything else? — Yes, (a croissant and an egg sandwich), please. / No, that's all, thanks.

Eat in or take away? — Eat in, please. / Take away, please.

OK, that's (£8.60), please. — Thank you very much. / Thanks a lot.

You're welcome.

Language Summary 4

VOCABULARY

4.1 ▶ Phrases with *like, have, live, work, study* 4A **1** p30

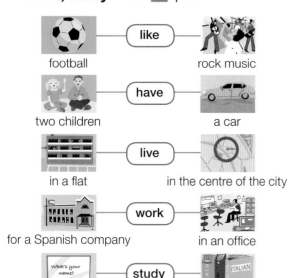

- football — like — rock music
- two children — have — a car
- in a flat — live — in the centre of the city
- for a Spanish company — work — in an office
- English — study — languages

TIP • a flat (UK) = an apartment (US)

4.2 ▶ Free time activities 4B **1** p32

watch TV or DVDs

go shopping

go to the cinema

go out with friends

eat out

play tennis

go to concerts

play video games

TIPS • We can say *I (watch TV) a lot.*, etc.
• *video games = computer games*

4.3 ▶ Things to buy 4C **1** p34

a magazine   tissues   a map   a newspaper   a postcard

chewing gum   a birthday card   batteries   sweets   a box of chocolates

TIP • The plural of *box* is *boxes*. The singular of *batteries* is *a battery*.

4.4 ▶ *this, that, these, those* 4C **2** p34

	here ↓	there →
singular	this	that
plural	these	those

How much is **this** map?
How much are **these** birthday cards?
How much is **that** big box of chocolates?
How much are **those** batteries?

TIP • *This*, *that*, *these*, *those* go before the noun: *How much is **this map**?*, ***These bags** are beautiful.*

4.5 ▶ Days of the week 4D **1** p36

Monday Tuesday
Wednesday Thursday Friday
Saturday Sunday

TIP • Saturday and Sunday = *the weekend*

4.6 ▶ Time words 4D **2** p36

60 **seconds** = 1 **minute**
60 minutes = 1 **hour**
24 hours = 1 **day**
7 days = 1 **week**
365 days = 1 **year**
12 **months** = 1 **year**

TIPS • 30 minutes = half an hour
• 15 minutes = quarter of an hour
• 18 months = a year and a half
• We say *two and a half years* not ~~*two years and a half*~~.

4.1 ▶ Present Simple (*I, you, we, they*): positive and negative 4A 3 p31

POSITIVE (+)

I **work** for a mobile phone company.
You **study** English.
We **live** in a very nice flat.
They **like** rock music.

TIP • The Present Simple positive is the same for *I, you, we* and *they*.

NEGATIVE (–)

I	don't	have	a new phone.	(don't =
You	don't	study	Russian.	do not)
We	don't	live	in Mexico City.	
They	don't	like	Chinese food.	

TIP • The Present Simple negative is the same for *I, you, we* and *they*.

4.2 ▶ Present Simple (*I, you, we, they*): questions and short answers

4B 5 p32

WH- QUESTIONS (?)

Where	do	you	live	in the UK?
What music	do	you	like?	
What	do	you	do	in your free time?
What food	do	you	like?	

TIP • We can say *What do you do?* to ask about a person's job:
A *What do you do?*
B *I'm a doctor.*

YES / NO QUESTIONS (?)	SHORT ANSWERS
Do I **know** you?	Yes, you **do**. No, you **don't**.
Do you **like** London?	Yes, I **do**. No, I **don't**.
Do we **have** a class today?	Yes, we/you **do**. No, we/you **don't**.
Do you **go** to concerts?	Yes, we **do**. No, we **don't**.
Do they **like** Chinese food?	Yes, they **do**. No, they **don't**.

TIPS • Present Simple questions are the same for *I, you, we* and *they*.
• We don't use *like, have*, etc. in short answers:
A *Do you like London?*
B *Yes, I do.* not ~~Yes, I like.~~ or ~~Yes, I do like.~~

4.1 ▶ In a shop 4C 6 p35

CUSTOMER	ASSISTANT
Excuse me. Do you have any (maps of London)?	Yes, they're over there.
How much is (this map)?	It's (£5.75).
How much are (these birthday cards)?	They're (£1.79) each.
Can I have (that box of chocolates) and (these cards), please?	Sure. Anything else?
Yes, (these sweets), please. No, that's all, thanks.	OK, that's (£12.33).
Here you are.	Thanks a lot. Thanks very much.

4.2 ▶ Telling the time 4D 3 4 p36

six o'clock / six   five past six   ten past six   quarter past six / six fifteen

twenty past six   twenty-five past six   half past six / six thirty   twenty-five to seven

twenty to seven   quarter to seven / six forty-five   ten to seven   five to seven

TIPS • We can say *quarter past / to …* or *a quarter past / to … .*
• We can also say the time like this: *six twenty, six fifty-five*, etc.

4.3 ▶ Talking about the time 4D 7 p36

| What time is it, please? | It's twenty to three. |

| What time is your English class? | It's at half past eight. |

TIPS • We can say *What time is it?* or *What's the time?*.
• We use ***at*** for times: *My class is at four o'clock.*
• a.m. = 0.00–12.00; p.m. = 12.00–24.00

Language Summary 5

VOCABULARY

5.1 ▸ Daily routines   5A **1** p38

get up   have breakfast   leave home

start work   have lunch   finish work

get home   have dinner   go to bed   sleep

5.2 ▸ Time phrases with *on*, *in*, *at*

5B **1** p40

on	in	at
Sunday	the morning	six o'clock
Monday	the afternoon	half past ten
Tuesday morning	the evening	midday
Friday afternoon	the week	midnight
Saturday evening		night
		the weekend

TIPS • We say *in the morning / afternoon / evening*, but *at night* not ~~in the night~~.
• *midday* = 12.00, *midnight* = 24.00

5.3 ▸ Food and drink (3)   5C **1** p42

chicken salad   vegetable lasagne   burger and chips   mushroom pizza

apple pie and cream   fruit salad   chocolate ice cream   strawberry ice cream   vanilla ice cream

a bottle of still mineral water   a bottle of sparkling mineral water   an orange juice   a coffee   a tea

5.4 ▸ Frequency adverbs and phrases with *every*

5D **1** **4** p44

FREQUENCY ADVERBS

always	usually	sometimes	not usually	never
100%				0%

PHRASES WITH *EVERY*

● We can use ***every*** + **time word**: *every day, every week, every month, every year*, etc.

TIPS • We say *every day* not ~~every days~~, *every week* not ~~every weeks~~, etc.
• We can also say *every morning, every afternoon, every evening, every night, every Sunday, every Friday evening, every six weeks, every four years*, etc.

WORD ORDER

● **Frequency adverbs** go after ***be***: *I'm **always** tired on Sundays. It's **not usually** very busy.*

● **Frequency adverbs** go before other **verbs**: *I **never have** breakfast. I **usually watch** sport on TV.*

● **Phrases with *every*** are usually at the end of the sentence: *I work in a hotel **every Saturday**. I play football **every Sunday morning**.*

TIP • We can say: *I'm always tired on **Sunday / Sundays**.*

5.1 ▶ Present Simple (*he, she, it*): positive and negative   5A 4 p39

POSITIVE (+)

- In positive sentences with *he, she* and *it* we add **-s** or **-es** to the verb: *She leave**s** home at 8.15. He watch**es** TV in the evening. It finish**es** at midnight.*

spelling rule	examples
most verbs: add **-s**	like**s** leave**s** work**s** get**s** sleep**s**
verbs ending in *-ch* or *-sh*: add **-es**	watch**es** teach**es** finish**es**
verbs ending in consonant + *y*: *y* → **-ies**	stud**ies**
the verbs *go* and *do*: add **-es**	goe**s** doe**s**
the verb *have* is irregular	**has**

NEGATIVE (–)

He	**doesn't**	**have**	a car.	(**doesn't** = does not)
She	**doesn't**	**like**	mornings.	
She	**doesn't**	**watch**	TV after dinner.	
It	**doesn't**	**start**	today.	

TIP • The Present Simple negative is the same for *he, she* and *it*: **He** *doesn't have a car.* **It** *doesn't start today.*

5.2 ▶ Present Simple (*he, she, it*): questions and short answers   5B 4 p41

WH- QUESTIONS (?)

Where	does	Nadine	**work**	at the weekend?
What	does	she	**do**	in the week?
Where	does	she	**live**	in Manchester?
What	does	she	**do**	in her free time?
When	does	he	**get up**	on Sunday?
When	does	it	**start**?	

TIPS • Present Simple questions are the same for *he, she* and *it*.
• We say *Where does Nadine work at the weekend?* not ~~*Where does Nadine works at the weekend?*~~.

YES / NO QUESTIONS (?)	SHORT ANSWERS
Does he **know** Nadine?	Yes, he **does**. No, he **doesn't**.
Does she **like** Manchester?	Yes, she **does**. No, she **doesn't**.
Does it **start** at 7.30?	Yes, it **does**. No, it **doesn't**.

- We use **does** in questions with *he, she* and *it*.
- We use **do** in questions with *I, you, we* and *they*.

TIP • We don't use *know*, etc. in short answers: **A** *Does he know her?* **B** *Yes, he does.* not ~~*Yes, he knows.*~~ or ~~*Yes, he does know.*~~

5.1 ▶ In a restaurant   5C 4 p43

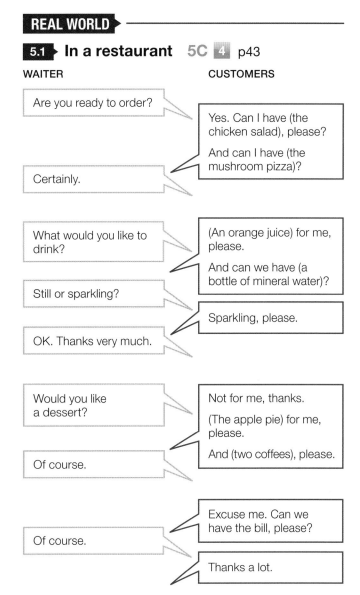

WAITER

CUSTOMERS

Are you ready to order?

Yes. Can I have (the chicken salad), please?

And can I have (the mushroom pizza)?

Certainly.

What would you like to drink?

(An orange juice) for me, please.

And can we have (a bottle of mineral water)?

Still or sparkling?

Sparkling, please.

OK. Thanks very much.

Would you like a dessert?

Not for me, thanks.

(The apple pie) for me, please.

And (two coffees), please.

Of course.

Excuse me. Can we have the bill, please?

Of course.

Thanks a lot.

TIP • We can use *the* or *a* when we order food: *Can I have **the** / **a** chicken salad, please? And can I have **the** / **a** mushroom pizza?*

Language Summary 6

VOCABULARY

6.1 ▶ Places in a town or city (1)
6A **1** p46

a park

a station

a theatre

a building

a river

an airport

a bus station

a museum

a shopping centre

TIP • *a station = a train station*

6.2 ▶ Places in a town or city (2)
6B **1** p48

a bank

a chemist's

a road

a cashpoint / an ATM

a bus stop

a supermarket

a square

a market

a post office

6.3 ▶ Things in your bag (2) 6C **1** p50

1 a map
2 a purse
3 a camera
4 keys
5 a laptop
6 a passport
7 a guide book
8 a wallet
9 an ID card
10 a credit card
11 money

6.4 ▶ Clothes 6D **1** p52

1	a shirt	4	trousers	7	boots	10	jeans	13	a coat
2	a tie	5	a jumper	8	a jacket	11	trainers	14	shoes
3	a suit	6	a skirt	9	a T-shirt	12	a dress		

TIPS • We can say **a pair of** *trousers / jeans / shoes / trainers / boots.*

• *Clothes* is a plural word: *Your clothes* **are** *over there.*

6.5 ▶ Colours 6D **2** p52

black   **white**   **yellow**   **brown**   **red**   **blue**   **grey**   **pink**   **green**

TIP • We use **What colour is / are ... ?** to ask about colours:
What colour is *Wayne's tie?* **What colour are** *Monica's boots?*

6.6 ▶ *favourite* 6D 6 p52

- *favourite* = the thing or person we like best

My **favourite** colour is pink.
This is my **favourite** jacket.
These are my **favourite** boots.
What's your **favourite** colour?
Who's your **favourite** actor?

TIP • We use *Who* to ask about a person:
A *Who's your favourite actor?*
B *Leonardo DiCaprio.*

My favourite colour is pink!

GRAMMAR

6.1 ▶ *a, some, a lot of; there is / there are*: positive 6A 4 p47

A, SOME, A LOT OF

There's **a person** in the park.

There are **some people** in the park.

There are **a lot of people** in the park.

- We use **a** or **an** with singular nouns: *a person*, *an airport*, etc.
- We use **some** and **a lot of** with plural nouns: *some museums*, *a lot of restaurants*, etc.

TIP • We can say *a lot of* or *lots of*: There are **lots of** people in the park.

THERE IS / THERE ARE
POSITIVE (+)

SINGULAR	**There's** a big new shopping centre. **There's** an airport in Bristol.
PLURAL	**There are** five theatres. **There are** some very nice parks. **There are** a lot of old buildings.

TIPS • there's = there is
• We write *there are* not ~~there're~~.

6.2 ▶ *there is / there are*: negative, *yes / no* questions and short answers; *any*

6B 3 p49

NEGATIVE (−)

There isn't a station near here.
There aren't any good restaurants near here.

YES / NO QUESTIONS (?)	SHORT ANSWERS
Is there a bank?	Yes, **there is**. No, **there isn't**.
Are there any shops?	Yes, **there are**. No, **there aren't**.

TIP • We say *Yes, there is.* not ~~Yes, there's~~.

ANY

- We use **any** in **negatives** and **questions** with *there are*:
  There aren't **any** *good restaurants near here.*
  Are there **any** *shops?*

TIP • We use **some** in **positive** sentences with *there are*:
There are **some** *very nice restaurants in the centre.*

REAL WORLD

6.1 ▶ At a tourist information centre

6C 4 p51

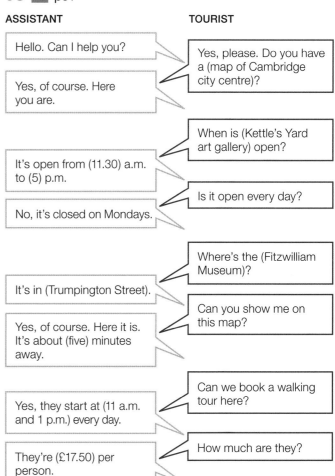

ASSISTANT	TOURIST
Hello. Can I help you?	Yes, please. Do you have a (map of Cambridge city centre)?
Yes, of course. Here you are.	
	When is (Kettle's Yard art gallery) open?
It's open from (11.30) a.m. to (5) p.m.	Is it open every day?
No, it's closed on Mondays.	
	Where's the (Fitzwilliam Museum)?
It's in (Trumpington Street).	Can you show me on this map?
Yes, of course. Here it is. It's about (five) minutes away.	
	Can we book a walking tour here?
Yes, they start at (11 a.m. and 1 p.m.) every day.	How much are they?
They're (£17.50) per person.	

125

Language Summary 7

VOCABULARY

7.1 ▶ Things you like and don't like
7A 1 p54

animals

classical music

visiting new places

horror films

watching sport on TV

shopping for clothes

soap operas

dancing

flying

TIP • UK: *a film* = US: *a movie*

7.2 ▶ *love, like, don't like, hate* 7A 3 p54

I love …   I like …   I don't like …   I hate …

- After *love*, *like*, *don't like* and *hate* we can use a **noun** or **verb+ing**.
  I love **animals**.   I don't like **dancing**.
  I like **soap operas**.   I hate **shopping** for clothes.

SPELLING OF VERB+*ING* FORMS

- Most verbs: *visit* → *visit**ing***, *watch* → *watch**ing***, *fly* → *fly**ing***, etc.
- Verbs ending in -e: *dance* → *danc**ing*** (not *danceing*), etc.
- Verbs ending in consonant + vowel + consonant: *shop* → *shop**ping*** (not *shoping*), etc.
- Verbs ending in -y: *play* → *play**ing*** (not *playying*), etc.

TIP • We don't use *the* when we talk about things we like or don't like in general: *I love animals.* (= all animals), *I don't like sport.* (= all sport).

7.3 ▶ Abilities 7B 1 p56

ski

ride a bike

drive

swim

speak German

play the piano

sing

play the guitar

play basketball

cook

TIPS • We say *play basketball / football / tennis* but *play **the** piano / **the** guitar*.
- *a bike* = *a bicycle*

7.4 ▶ Prepositions of place 7C 2 p58

The café is **on** the left.

The café is **on** the right.

The café is **in** King Street.

The café is **opposite** the bank.

The café is **next to** the bank.

The café is **near** the bank.

TIP • We can say ***in** King Street* or ***on** King Street*.

Things people do online 7D 1 p60

send emails
get / receive emails

buy things online
sell things online

read a blog
write a blog

watch TV programmes
watch videos

be on Facebook
be on Twitter

download videos
download music
download apps

book hotels
book holidays
book flights

listen to the radio
listen to music

chat to friends and family

search for information

TIPS • online = connected to the internet: *Do you chat to friends online?*
• *a TV programme (UK) = a TV show (US)*

GRAMMAR

7.1 **Object pronouns** 7A 8 p55

• Look at these sentences. Notice the word order.
Subject pronouns go **before** the verb.
Object pronouns go **after** the verb.

subject	verb	object
I	love	soap operas.
Adam	hates	them.

subject pronouns	I	you	he	she	it	we	they
object pronouns	me	you	him	her	it	us	them

7.2 *can*: **positive and negative** 7B 3 p56

• We use **can** or **can't** to talk about ability.
• *Can* and *can't* are the same for *I, you, he, she, it, we* and *they*.

POSITIVE (+)

She	can	play	the piano.
They	can	ski.	

NEGATIVE (−)

I	can't	swim.	
We	can't	speak	Chinese.

TIPS • We sometimes use (**very**) **well** with *can*:
*She can swim **well**. They can ski **very well**.*
• We say *She can play the piano.* not ~~She can to play the piano.~~

7.3 *can*: *yes / no* **questions and short answers** 7B 8 p57

YES / NO QUESTIONS (?)	SHORT ANSWERS
Can you **cook**?	Yes, I **can**. No, I **can't**.
Can he **play** the guitar?	Yes, he **can**. No, he **can't**.
Can she **speak** French?	Yes, she **can**. No, she **can't**.
Can they **swim**?	Yes, they **can**. No, they **can't**.

TIP • We don't use *do* or *does* in questions with *can*:
Can you cook? not ~~Do you can cook?~~

REAL WORLD

7.1 **Asking for and giving directions** 7C 6 p59

ASKING FOR DIRECTIONS

Excuse me. Where's the (museum)?

Excuse me. Is there a (bank) near here?

GIVING DIRECTIONS

Go along this road and turn left.

Go along this road and turn right.

That's (Park Street).

The (museum) is on the right, next to the (theatre).

The (bank) is on the left, opposite the (station).

It's over there, near the (cinema).

TIP • We can say *on **the** right / left* or *on **your** right / left*.

Language Summary 8

VOCABULARY

8.1 ▶ Adjectives (2) 8A 1 p62

short   long

terrible   great
awful   fantastic
            amazing

right   wrong

difficult   easy

interesting   boring

happy   unhappy

old   young

full   empty

8.2 ▶ Years and past time phrases 8B 1 2 p64

YEARS

1887 = eighteen eighty-seven

1900 = nineteen hundred

1980 = nineteen eighty

2000 = two thousand

2009 = two thousand and nine

2010 = twenty ten

TIPS • For the years 2000–2009, we usually say *two thousand*, *two thousand and one*, etc.

• For the years 2010–2099, we usually say *twenty ten*, *twenty eleven*, etc.

• We use *in* with years: *in 1980*, *in 2009*, etc.

PAST TIME PHRASES

Joe was in Paris **last** week.

He was in bed four hours **ago**.

He was at home **yesterday** afternoon.

He's at work **now**.

TIPS • We use *last* with days (*last Monday*) and months (*last June*).

• We also say *last night*, *last week*, *last weekend*, *last month*, *last year*.

• We say *yesterday morning*, *yesterday afternoon* and *yesterday evening*, but *last night* not ~~yesterday night~~.

• *four hours **ago*** = four hours before now

8.3 ▶ Months and dates

8C 1 2 p66

MONTHS

January	May	September
February	June	October
March	July	November
April	August	December

TIPS • We use capital letters with months.

• We use *in* with months: *in January*, etc.

DATES

1st	first	16th	sixteenth
2nd	second	17th	seventeenth
3rd	third	18th	eighteenth
4th	fourth	19th	nineteenth
5th	fifth	20th	twentieth
6th	sixth	21st	twenty-first
7th	seventh	22nd	twenty-second
8th	eighth	23rd	twenty-third
9th	ninth	24th	twenty-fourth
10th	tenth	25th	twenty-fifth
11th	eleventh	26th	twenty-sixth
12th	twelfth	27th	twenty-seventh
13th	thirteenth	28th	twenty-eighth
14th	fourteenth	29th	twenty-ninth
15th	fifteenth	30th	thirtieth
		31st	thirty-first

8.4 ▶ Big numbers 8D 1 p68

150 = a hundred and fifty

390 = three hundred and ninety

1,000 = a thousand

16,200 = sixteen thousand, two hundred

750,000 = seven hundred and fifty thousand

1,000,000 = a million

50,000,000 = fifty million

TIPS • We don't use a plural *-s* with *hundred*, *thousand* or *million*: *three hundred* not ~~three hundreds~~, etc.

• We use *and* after *hundred*, but not after *thousand*: *a hundred **and** fifty*, but *sixteen thousand, two hundred*.

• We can say *a hundred* or ***one** hundred*, *a thousand* or ***one** thousand* and *a million* or ***one** million*.

8.1 ► Past Simple of *be*: positive and negative   8A 3 p63

POSITIVE (+)	NEGATIVE (−)
I **was**	I **wasn't** (= was not)
you **were**	you **weren't** (= were not)
he / she / it **was**	he / she / it **wasn't**
we **were**	we **weren't**
they **were**	they **weren't**

I **was** at the World Cup Final.
We **were** near the Opera House.
The stadium **wasn't** full.
They **weren't** very happy.

TIP • The past of *there is / there are* is *there was / there were*:
There was a big party. **There were** some amazing fireworks.

8.2 ► Past Simple of *be*: questions and short answers; *was born / were born*   8B 5 p65

WH- QUESTIONS (?)

Where	**was**	I / he / she / it last week?
When	**were**	you / we / they in India?

Where		**was**	the wedding?
How old		**were**	Sunil and Pria?
How many people		**were**	at the wedding?
Where		**was**	Sunil's sister?

YES / NO QUESTIONS (?)	SHORT ANSWERS
Was I / he / she / it at the wedding?	Yes, I / he / she / it **was**. No, I / he / she / it **wasn't**.
Were you / we / they at the wedding?	Yes, you / we / they **were**. No, you / we / they **weren't**.

TIP • We can also make questions with *Was there … ?* and *Were there … ?*: **Was there** a party? **Were there** a lot of people at the wedding?

WAS BORN / WERE BORN

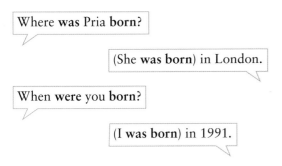

Where **was** Pria **born**?

(She **was born**) in London.

When **were** you **born**?

(I **was born**) in 1991.

TIP • We say *I was born in 1991.* not *I borned in 1991.*

8.1 ► Talking about days and dates   8C 3 p66

What day is it today?

(It's) Monday.

What's the date today?

(It's) March **the seventh**.

When's your birthday?

(It's **on**) June **the second**.

TIPS • We can say *March **the** seventh* or ***the** seventh of March*.
• We write *March 7th* or *7th March*.
• In the UK, **5/6/15** = 5th June 2015 (day / month / year).
In the USA, **5/6/15** = 6th May 2015 (month / day / year).

8.2 ► Making suggestions   8C 8 p67

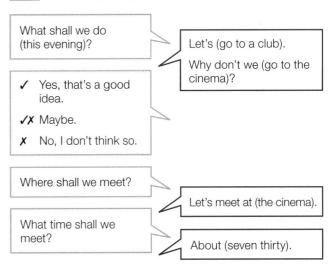

What shall we do (this evening)?

Let's (go to a club). Why don't we (go to the cinema)?

✓ Yes, that's a good idea.
✓✗ Maybe.
✗ No, I don't think so.

Where shall we meet?

Let's meet at (the cinema).

What time shall we meet?

About (seven thirty).

TIPS • We use *Let's … , Why don't we …. ?* and *Shall we … ?* to make suggestions.
• We use *What / Where / What time shall we … ?* to ask for suggestions.
• *Let's … , Why don't we … ?* and *Shall we … ?* are followed by a verb: *Let's **go** to the cinema.* etc.

Language Summary 9

VOCABULARY

9.1 ▶ Transport 9A **1** p70

a car

a bus

a train

a taxi

a bike

a motorbike

a plane

a boat

TIPS • We can say *a taxi* or *a cab*.
• We say *I go / come / travel **by** car*, **by** *bus*, etc.: *I usually go to work **by** car*.
• We also say: *I **walk** to work / school*, etc.
• *go by plane = fly, go by car = drive, go by bike = cycle*

9.2 ▶ Holiday activities

9B **1** p72

Match phrases 1–11 to pictures a–k.

1 [e] go on holiday
2 [ ] take photos
3 [ ] go to the beach
4 [ ] stay with friends or family
5 [ ] stay in a hotel
6 [ ] go sightseeing
7 [ ] go swimming
8 [ ] go for a walk
9 [ ] rent a car
10 [ ] travel around
11 [ ] have a good time

TIP • *go on holiday* (UK) = *go on vacation* (US)

9.3 ▶ At the station 9C **1** p74

a customer   a ticket office

a ticket machine

a platform

a single

a return

TIP • *a single* = a single ticket, *a return* = a return ticket

9.4 ▶ Question words 9D **4** p77

QUESTION WORD	ASKS ABOUT ...	EXAMPLE
Who	a person	**Who**'s she?
What	a thing	**What**'s that?
When	a time	**When** do you start work?
Where	a place	**Where** does he live?
Why	a reason	**Why** are you tired?
How old	age	**How old** are they?
How many	a number	**How many** people are there?
How much	an amount of money	**How much** are those shoes?

TIPS • We also use ***What time ... ?*** to ask about a time:
A *What time do you go to bed?* **B** *At half past eleven.*
• We usually answer *Why ... ?* questions with ***Because ...*** :
A *Why are you tired?* **B** *Because I got up at 5 a.m.*

a

b

c

d

e

f

g

h

i

j

k

9.1 Past Simple: positive 9A [5] p71

REGULAR VERBS

- To make the Past Simple of regular verbs, we usually add **-ed** to the verb: want**ed**, start**ed**, visit**ed**, etc.
- For regular verbs ending in *-e* (*like*, *arrive*, etc.), we add **-d** to the verb: lik**ed**, arriv**ed**, etc.

TIPS • The Past Simple of *travel* is travel**led**.
• The Past Simple of *study* is stud**ied**.

REGULAR VERBS IN UNITS 1–10

arrive ask book chat check cook download
finish hate help like listen live look love
move play practise receive rent repeat
search show start stay turn use visit walk
want watch work

IRREGULAR VERBS

- Many verbs in English are irregular. There are no spelling rules for irregular verbs.

IRREGULAR VERBS IN UNITS 1–10

verb	Past Simple	verb	Past Simple
buy	bought	put	put
choose	chose	read /riːd/	read /red/
come	came	ride	rode
do	did	say	said /sed/
drink	drank	see	saw /sɔː/
drive	drove	sell	sold
eat	ate	send	sent
feel	felt	sing	sang
find	found	sleep	slept
fly	flew	speak	spoke
get	got	spend	spent
give	gave	swim	swam
go	went	take	took
have	had	teach	taught /tɔːt/
hear	heard /hɜːd/	tell	told
know	knew	think	thought /θɔːt/
leave	left	understand	understood
make	made	wear	wore
meet	met	write	wrote

TIPS • The Past Simple of regular and irregular verbs is the same for *I*, *you*, *he*, *she*, *it*, *we* and *they*.
• The Past Simple of *be* is *was* or *were*.

9.2 Past Simple: negative 9B [4] p72

I	didn't	stay	in a hotel.
He	didn't	go	swimming.
She	didn't	visit	any other places.
We	didn't	go	on holiday last year.
They	didn't	stay	there for very long.

(**didn't** = did not)

9.3 Past Simple: questions and short answers 9B [8] p73

WH- QUESTIONS (?)

Where	did	Heidi	**go**	on holiday?
Who	did	she	**stay**	with?
When	did	Charlie	**go**	to the beach?
How many photos	did	they	**take**?	

YES / NO QUESTIONS (?)	**SHORT ANSWERS**
Did he **go** swimming?	Yes, he **did**. No, he **didn't**.
Did they **visit** Turkey last year?	Yes, they **did**. No, they **didn't**.

TIPS • Past Simple questions are the same for *I*, *you*, *he*, *she*, *it*, *we* and *they*.
• We don't use *did* in questions with *was* and *were*.
• Notice the difference between negatives and questions in the Present Simple and Past Simple:

PRESENT SIMPLE	**PAST SIMPLE**
I **don't** live in a flat.	I **didn't** live in a flat.
He **doesn't** have a car.	He **didn't** have a car.
Where **do** you work?	Where **did** you work?
Where **does** she live?	Where **did** she live?

REAL WORLD

9.1 Buying train tickets 9C [3] p74

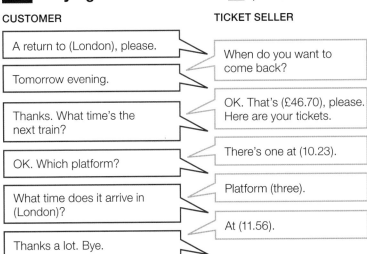

CUSTOMER	TICKET SELLER
A return to (London), please.	When do you want to come back?
Tomorrow evening.	OK. That's (£46.70), please. Here are your tickets.
Thanks. What time's the next train?	There's one at (10.23).
OK. Which platform?	Platform (three).
What time does it arrive in (London)?	At (11.56).
Thanks a lot. Bye.	

9.2 Asking about the weekend 9C [9] p75

Did you have a good weekend?
What did you do at the weekend?
Where did you go?
What did you do there?

Did you have a good time?
What did you see?
Did you enjoy it?

Language Summary 10

VOCABULARY

10.1 Future plans 10A 1 p78

- **start** < school or university / a new job
- **leave** < school or university / your job
- **do** < a (computer) course / an exam
- **move** < house / to another city or country
- **get** < engaged / married
- **look for** < a house or a flat / a (new) job

do an exam

move house

get married

look for a new job

10.2 Future time phrases 10A 7 p79

tonight
tomorrow morning
next week
next month
in June next year
in 2025

TIPS • We say *tonight* not ~~this night~~.

• We can say *tomorrow morning*, *tomorrow afternoon*, *tomorrow evening* and *tomorrow night*.

• We use *next* in these phrases: *next week*, *next weekend*, *next month*, *next year*.

• We use *in* with months (*in June*) and years (*in 2025*).

• We can also use *next* with months (*next June*) and days (*next Monday*).

• We use *on* with days (*on Monday*).

10.3 Phrases with *have*, *watch*, *go*, *go to*
10B 1 p80

- **have** dinner with friends / coffee with friends / a party
- **watch** TV / the news / sport on TV
- **go** shopping / swimming / running
- **go to** the cinema / the gym / a party

have a party

watch the news

go running

go to the gym

10.4 Adjectives (3): feelings 10C 1 p82

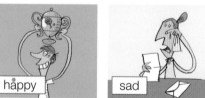
happy

sad

excited

angry

bored

hungry

tired

scared

TIP • We can say *I'm* excited, etc. or *I feel* excited, etc.

10.1 *be going to*: positive and negative

10A 3 p79

● We use *be going to* + *verb* to talk about **future plans**.

POSITIVE (+)

I	'm (= am)	going to	do	a computer course.
He / She	's (= is)	going to	leave	his / her job.
We / You / They	're (= are)	going to	travel	around the UK.

NEGATIVE (–)

I	'm not	going to	start	university this year.
He / She	isn't	going to	stay	here for very long.
We / You / They	aren't	going to	live	in São Paulo.

TIPS ● With the verb *go* we usually say: *I'm going to the cinema.* not *I'm going to go to the cinema.* But both sentences are correct.

● We can also say: *He's not going to* … , *She's not going to* … , *We're not going to* … , *You're not going to* … and *They're not going to* … .

10.2 *be going to*: questions and short answers

10B 4 p80

WH- QUESTIONS (?)

What	am	I		going to	do	tomorrow?
Where	are	you / we / they		going to	live?	
When	is	he / she		going to	move	to South Africa?

When **is** Rosie **going to move** to South Africa?
What **is** her husband **going to do** there?
Where **are** her brothers **going to live**?
What **is** Andy **going to do** this evening?

YES / NO QUESTIONS (?)	SHORT ANSWERS
Are you **going to see** a film?	Yes, I **am**. No, I'm **not**.
Is he / she **going to look for** a job?	Yes, he / she **is**. No, he / she **isn't**.
Are you **going to sell** your flat?	Yes, we **are**. No, we **aren't**.
Are they **going to have** a party?	Yes, they **are**. No, they **aren't**.

TIP ● We can also say: *No, he's not.*, *No, she's not.*, *No, we're not.* and *No, they're not.*

10.1 Saying goodbye and good luck   10C 5 p83

Have a good journey.

Thanks a lot.

Have a good	journey. holiday. day. weekend. birthday. time.

See you in September.

Yes, see you.

See you	in (September). in (two hours). this (evening). on (Monday). soon. later.

Good luck with your driving test.

Thanks very much.

Good luck with your	new job. driving test. exam. new school. English test.

Phonemic Symbols

Vowel sounds

/ə/	/æ/	/ʊ/	/ɒ/	/ɪ/	/i/	/e/	/ʌ/
computer	bag man	book good	coffee hot	six thing	happy easy	bed any	much son

/ɜː/	/ɑː/	/uː/	/ɔː/	/iː/			
burger girl	father car	blue who	forty water	eat meet			

/eə/	/ɪə/	/ʊə/	/ɔɪ/	/aɪ/	/eɪ/	/əʊ/	/aʊ/
chair where	near we're	tourist	boy noisy	nine my	eight day	go know	out brown

Consonant sounds

/p/	/b/	/f/	/v/	/t/	/d/	/k/	/g/
park shop	be bike	five left	very live	time white	dog red	cold look	girl bag

/θ/	/ð/	/tʃ/	/dʒ/	/s/	/z/	/ʃ/	/ʒ/
three think	mother the	chips much	orange juice	suit city	zero days	shirt sugar	television

/m/	/n/	/ŋ/	/h/	/l/	/r/	/w/	/j/
me name	now train	sing think	here hello	leave plane	read price	waiter we	you yes

Answer Key

1D 7 p96

3 tables; 5 men; 2 women; 10 books; 3 pens; 8 pencils; 7 apples; 4 bags; 6 mobiles

2A 9 b p15

3 Leonardo DiCaprio isn't Italian. He's American.
4 Nissan isn't a Chinese company. It's a Japanese company.
5 ✓
6 The White House isn't in New York. It's in Washington.
7 Prince William isn't Russian. He's British.
8 ✓
9 Fiat isn't a French company. It's an Italian company.
10 ✓

2D 10 p21

Amybeth 24; Richard 58; Lucinda 22
Adela 47; Dagmar 76
Joe 13; Alexander 16
Luke 35; Jessica 41; Maggie 71;
Salvador 3; Alec 5; Belle 2
Jean 80; Don 87; Chris 51

Classroom Instructions

Listen.

Read.

Write.

Look at the photo.

Work in pairs.

Work in groups.

Match.

Fill in the gaps.

Compare answers.

Listen and check.

Listen and practise.

Ask and answer the questions.

Self-study DVD-ROM Instructions

What's on the Self-study DVD-ROM?

- over 300 exercises to practise all language areas
- a Review Video for each unit
- *My Tests* and *My Progress* sections
- an interactive Phonemic Symbols chart
- an e-Portfolio with *Grammar Reference*, *Word List* and *Word Cards* practice tool, plus a *My Work* section where you can build a digital portfolio of your work
- the main audio recordings from the Student's Book

Use the navigation b\[ar\] to go to different are\[as\] of the DVD-ROM.

Choose a unit.

Practise the new language from each lesson.

Listen and practise new language. You can also record your own pronunciation.

Watch the Review Video and do the activities.

Create vocabulary and grammar tests for language in the Student's Book.

Listen to the main recordings from the Student's Book and read the scripts.

Go to the home screen.

Get help on using the Self-study DVD-ROM

Go to Cambridge Dictionaries Online.

Look at the Phonemic Symbols chart and practise the pronunciation of vowel and consonant sounds.

Check *My Progress* to see your scores for completed activities.

Explore the e-Portfolio.

System requirements

Windows
- Intel Pentium 4 2GHz or faster
- Microsoft® Windows® XP (SP3), Windows® Vista (SP2), Windows® 7 and Windows® 8
- Minimum 1GB RAM
- Minimum 750MB of hard drive space
- Adobe® Flash® Player 10.3.183.7 or later

Mac OS
- Intel Core™ Duo 1.83GHz or faster
- Mac OSX 10.5 or later
- Minimum 1GB RAM
- Minimum 750MB of hard drive space
- Adobe® Flash® Player 10.3.183.7 or later

Installing the Self-study DVD-ROM to your hard disk

- Insert the **face2face Second edition** Starter Self-study DVD-ROM into your CD/DVD drive. The DVD-ROM will automatically start to install. Follow the installation instructions on your screen.

- On a Windows PC, if the DVD-ROM does not automatically start to install, open **My Computer**, locate your CD/DVD drive and open it to view the contents of the DVD-ROM. Double-click on the *CambridgeApplicationInstaller* file. Follow the installation instructions on your screen.

- On a Mac, if the DVD-ROM does not automatically start to install, double-click on the **face2face** DVD icon on your desktop. Double-click on the *CambridgeApplicationInstaller* file. Follow the installation instructions on your screen.

Support

If you need help with installing the DVD-ROM, please visit: www.cambridge.org/elt/support